# Practical Understanding of Dewey Decimal Classification 22

Mohinder Kaur Gill

ATLANTIC
PUBLISHERS & DISTRIBUTORS (P) LTD

Published by
**ATLANTIC**
**PUBLISHERS & DISTRIBUTORS (P) LTD**
7/22, Ansari Road, Darya Ganj, New Delhi-110002
Phones : +91-11-40775252, 23273880, 23275880, 23280451
Fax : +91-11-23285873
Web : www.atlanticbooks.com
E-mail : orders@atlanticbooks.com

Branch Office
5, Nallathambi Street, Wallajah Road, Chennai-600002
Phones : +91-44-64611085, 32413319
E-mail : chennai@atlanticbooks.com



Printed in India at Nice Printing Press, A-33/3A, Site-IV, Industrial Area, Sahibabad, Ghaziabad, U.P.

# Preface

In this modern age of information and communication technology, classification is used almost in every field of life. In library, classification plays a vital role to save the time of the reader. If we classify the books with DDC and arrange them according to the class number on the shelves author wise, we can find them within seconds. For this reason, DDC is used in the libraries all over the world. Keeping in view the universal use of Dewey Decimal Classification, all the universities and colleges have included DDC as a subject in the courses of Library and Information Science in India as well as abroad.

This book is written to meet the requirements of the students who are preparing for their Library and Information Science courses and for librarians who are using DDC 22nd for their libraries. The book is written in simple language and lucid manner so as to make it comprehensible for the learners. Sufficient number of examples with explanations are given from schedules. So far as Computer Science is concerned, DDC 22nd has fulfilled the needs of librarians to classify these books in comparison of 19th edition. In some Indian universities web Dewey is also included in the syllabus.

The book will enable the students to make use of 1-6 tables with schedule numbers, and synthesize the numbers from different parts of schedules and tables.

I am thankful to the Indian as well as foreign authors whose books I have used to learn DDC 22nd. I am highly thankful to Ms. Mandeep Kaur (Intern) and Mrs. Kamlesh Sharma, Assistant Librarian for editing the book, and Mr. Jaspreet Singh Toor for typing the theory portion of the book.

I am highly thankful to my family living far away from the country. My in-laws, my husband Faujdeep Singh Gill, daughter Dr. Amardeep Kaur, and my son Arshdeep Singh have encouraged me throughout the time to complete this book. I am grateful to them.

There may be some shortcomings in the book, and I will welcome the suggestions from the readers.

**Mohinder Kaur Gill**
**E-mail:** mohinderkaur23@yahoo.com

# Contents

# 1

# Introduction

### Dewey Decimal Classification: 22nd Edition

DDC is the oldest and the most widely used in the Libraries of world. Melvil Dewey was born on 10 September 1851. His full name was Melvil Louis Dewey. At the age of 23, he was graduated from Amherst College in 1874. He became assistant college librarian. He worked as a student assistant in the college library in 1873 and since that time he began developing the first draft of his system for arranging books and got his classification scheme published in the year 1876. He became a leader in American librarianship and helped to found American Library Association (ALA) and first American Library School at Columbia University in 1887 and started teaching. Melvil was the editor and publisher of the first "Library Journal. He was also an advocate and spelling Reform."[1]

First edition of DDC was published under the name of "A Classification and Subject Index for Cataloguing and Arranging the Books and Pamphlets of a Library". It has 44 pages out of which 14 pages were of introduction. 1-15 editions of DDC were published in one volume each. 16th and 17th editions were published in two volumes. 18th and 19th editions were published in three volumes. 20th, 21st and 22nd editions are published in four volumes. 22nd edition was published in 2003 and it contains 4060 total pages.

### Structure of DDC 22

DDC 22nd edition is published by OCLC. OCLC online computer library center, Inc., Dublin: Ohio, 2003. It has four volumes, volume 1 has lxxvii, 731 pages; volume 2 has XVI,

1250 pages; volume 3 has 1074 pages and volume 4 has 928 pages, 3983 + 77 = 4060 pages.[2]

Volume 1: Manual Tables: It contains a forward by the decimal classification editorial policy committee (EPC). Volume 2 has Preface and Acknowledgement by Joan S. Mitchell, Editor-in-chief, DDC, OCLC, Inc., volume 3 contains new features in edition 2nd, volume 4 includes introduction to Dewey decimal classification, volume 5 has a glossary contains the terms and its meanings used in DDC 22, volume 6 Manual contains notes on table (1-6) numbers and notes on schedule numbers 000-999. It contains flow charts for building numbers of literature, Music, Geography & Travel, and Travelers and a flow chart for history. Then it contains tables 1-6. It contains the following tables 1-6.

**Table 1:** Standard subdivisions.

**Table 2:** Geographic areas, historical periods, persons.

**Table 3:** Subdivisions for arts, for individual literatures, for specific literary forms.

**Table 3A:** Subdivisions for works by or about individual authors.

**Table 3B:** Subdivisions for works by or about more than one author.

**Table 3C:** Notation to be added where instructed in Table 3B. (700.4, 791.4, 808-809)

**Table 4:** Subdivisions of manual languages and language families.

**Table 5:** Ethnic and National Groups.

**Table 6:** Languages, it also includes relocations and discontinuations and reused numbers.

**Volume 2 schedules (000-500)** and contains three summaries:

(1) The ten main classes (000-900)

(2) Second summary contains the hundred divisions of (000-990)

(3) Third summary contains the thousands sections of hundred divisions (000-999) and

**Volume 3:** Contains schedule from (600-900)

**Volume 4:** It contains relative index and abbreviations used in the index. There are some important notes in DDC 22nd edition.[3]

**Notes in DDC 22:** There are a number of major notes in the 22nd edition that tell us what is found in a class, what is found at other classes, including notes in standing rooms, notes that explain changes in schedules and tables, notes that instruct the classifier in number building, notes that prescribe citation order and notes that explain options.

### (A) Notes that describe what is found in a class

These notes include definition notes, scope notes, former heading notes, variant-name notes, class-here notes.

For example, of a scope note or a definition note is found at

553 – Economic Geology

The first note there reads, "Quantitative occurrence and distribution of geologic materials of economic utility." The second note in this classification is an example of a class-here note. "Class here interdisciplinary works on non-metallic geologic materials." Such notes are used to list major topics that are included at a class and also to indicate where interdisciplinary and comprehensive works are to be classified. Number built notes explain the source and process of constructing a number by adding notation from the tables and other parts of schedules to the base numbers. For example,

353.132 63 – Foreign Service

**Former Heading Notes:** These are given only when the heading associated with a class number in the previous edition has been altered to such a degree that the new heading bears little or no resemblance to the previous heading, even though the meaning of the number has remained substantially the same, e.g.

659.131 5 – Industrial Advertising

Former heading: Advertising Directed to Vocational

**Class-here Notes:** These topics may be broader or narrower than the heading, overlap it, or define another way of looking at essentially the same material. Topics in class-here notes are considered to approximate the whole of the class.

For example, 343.08 – Regulation of commerce, besides inclusion note. We read the instruction "class-here commodity exchanges". Such topics are generally broader than the class number or overlap other numbers and only for convenience are to be placed here. Standard subdivisions may be added for any topic in a class-here note.

**(B) Including notes (notes that identifies topics in "standing room")**

Including notes provide a location for topics that do not yet have enough works about them to justify a separate number. But whose literature may grow in the future and at which time they may be assigned their own number. Standing room notes begin with the word including. For example,

025.322 – Choice of entry and form of heading.

The first note says, "Including corporate headings, personal name headings, and uniform titles." There are already subdivision 025.322 2 – Authority files and it would be possible in the future those individual subdivisions for corporate headings, personal headings and uniform titles could be made.[4]

**(C) Notes that describe what is found in other classes**

1. **Class elsewhere notes** lead the classifier to interrelated topics or distinguish among numbers in the same notational hierarchy. All notes that begin with the word "class" are class elsewhere notes except when they begin with "class-here"

370.15 – Educational Psychology

Class interdisciplinary works on psychology in 150. Class psychology of a specific topic in education with the topic, plus notation 019 from table, e.g.

Psychology of special education = 371.901 9 (p. 1, V. 1)

371.9 + 019 = 371.901 9

155.4 – Child Psychology

Class interdisciplinary works on child development 305.231

2. **See reference number:** Treats a subject from various points of views. Throughout Table 2, see reference (often in foot note form) lead from the implied comprehensive number

for a Jurisdiction, region, or feature to its subordinate parts in other classes, e.g.

4115 = High Land

Class here *Scottish Highlands.

**3. See also references:** It leads the classifier to related topics. It appears in Italics.

584.3 – Liliidae

Class here Liliales, lilies

For orchidales, see 584.4

See also 583.29 for water lilies.

### (D) Notes that explaining changes in schedules and tables

Number building instructions provide ways to gain greater depth of analysis at a particular classification.

**Notes prescribe citation and preference order:** These notes help the classifier to decide which of more than one aspect or citation to use for classification.

Citation order allows the use of two or more facets in a specified order. Preference order tells the classifier to choose a facet where only one can choose, e.g.

011.1 – 011.8 General Bibliographies

Under other instructions are given, class a subject with aspects in two or more subdivisions of 011.1-001.8 in the number coming last, e.g.

Russian-Language newspapers on microfilm 011.36 (not 011.291 71 or 011.35)

**Option Notes:** Options always appear in parenthesis. These options may be of benefit in providing alternative methods for handling certain situations. Such kind of options are provided for religions, language and literatures to international classifiers, e.g.

Under 420-490 – Specific Languages

**Caption B:** To give local emphasis and a shorter number to a specific language, place it first by use of a letter or other symbol, e.g.

Arabic Language = 4A0

Similarly Under = 016 – Bibliography and catalogues of works on specific subjects or in specific discipline.

**Option:** Class with the specific discipline or subject, plus notation 016 from Table 1, e.g.

Bibliographies of Medicine = 016.610
= 016.61

**"Do not use" notes:** When a regular place of a S.S. is shifted wholly or partially to some other number. If a number is wholly shifted then such a number is enclosed in square brackets. We will find here "do not use, class in", e.g.

362.09 Historical, Geographic, Persons treatment.
Do not use; class in 362.9.[5]

## Changes in DDC 22nd Edition

DDC 22nd contains general major updates, many new numbers and topics and a few structural changes. Several new developments have been added and many classes have been revised and expanded but no schedule has been changed fundamentally.

## Major Updates in DDC 22nd Edition

There are two striking changes in DDC 22. Table 7 has been removed and replaced with direct use of notation already available in the schedule in notation 08 from Table 1. Secondly, each manual entry has been reviewed with an eye towards classifier efficiency. Basic instructions on the use of Dewey decimal classification have moved to the introduction. 004-006-Data processing and computer science have been completely updated.

Two edition plans to reduce Christian bias in 200 Religion was initiated in 21st edition. And 22nd ed. contains rest of the expansions. Specific aspects of religion moved from 291 to the 201-209, vacated in 21st edition. It includes expansions of Bahia faith at 297-938. These are revised and expanded in 299.6 for religions originating among black African and people of black African descent. 299.7-8 for religions of American native origin. Social groups (305) and (306) cultural institutions are revised and expanded.

(340) Law includes several improvements that relate to law of nations, inter-governmental organizations and human rights.

The most visible change in 510 Mathematics schedule is the use of 518 for numerical analysis drawn from different parts of 510.

In chemistry, analytical Chemistry (543) is revised, 544 qualitative analysis, 545 quantitative analysis and 547.3 analytical organic chemistry are relocated here and classes 544 and 545 have been vacated in DDC 22.

610 Medicine and health has updated and expanded developments throughout medicine.

At the request of many users and EPC History and geography has moved interdisciplinary and descriptive works on facilities for travelers from 647.94 to 910.46 and to specific area numbers in 913-919. In Cooperation with national libraries and translation partners, historical periods are updated throughout the 930-990. It also includes important new expansion for the holocaust at 940.531 8. The web version of DDC 22nd is available to web Dewey subscribers since June 2003 (15 June 2003).[6]

**Selected Changes in Table 1**

-029-Commercial Miscellany

Subdivisions discontinued to -029 & reused immediately for geographic treatment. Table 2 has updated geographic provisions developed with the advice of national libraries and translation partners.

Notation 3 from Table T3C has also been revised to provide a better arrangement closely parallels the grouping of topics in the DDC schedules themselves.

The name of Table 5 has changed from "Racial, Ethnics, National Groups" to "Ethnic and National Groups". Table 5 includes expanded provisions for American native people and Table 6 includes the corresponding expansion for American native language.

Table 7 has been removed and replaced with the direct use of notation already available in the schedule and in notation 08 from Table 1.

Basic instructions are moved in the introduction of DDC. Manual entries have revised in a consistent style to promote quick understanding & efficient Dewey decimal classification."[7]

("New: ACOC Seminar, Sydney, July 2003")

### Advantages

(1) Periodical revision of DDC is the big advantage in order to keep it up to date. (2) It brings the related subjects together on the shelf. (3) Indo Arabic Notation is used to assign class members. It's very simple and easy to remember. (4) Its relative index brings together different aspects of the same subjects that are scattered in the different disciplines. (5) It is able to accommodate new subjects of the future because of infinite expression and subdivision. (6) Most of the libraries are using DDC to organize library materials.

### Disadvantages

No doubt, DDC is biased towards American & European languages, Literature, History and Religion. Deep Classification results in long members, which are difficult to write on spine labels. When new editions come, some old numbers are changed & altering of numbers creates number of new problems like reclassification, relabelling and resheliving. Some related disciplines are scattered like languages and literatures, Social Sciences and History. In literature, literary works of a same author are scattered according to form. For example, Shakespeare's poems are separated from his plays.

DDC is used almost in all the libraries of the world because of its simple and easy notation and it has the capacity to accommodate the new subjects and disciplines of the future. As, with 22nd edition we are able to assign classification numbers to all the titles of computer science in comparison of 19th edition. This is the best scheme to classify and organize any kind of reading material on the shelves of our libraries in a logical way.[8]

### Notes

1. Taylor, Arlene G., "Introduction to Cataloguing and Classification" 10th ed., Chapter 15, *Decimal Classification*, mss, 2005, p. 1.

2. Satija, M.P., Dewey decimal classification: exercises in the 22nd edition, New Delhi: Ess Ess, 2004, pp. 1-3.
3. Dewey Decimal Classification and Relative Index: /devised by Melvil Dewey. 22nd /edited by John s. Mitchell et al., Dublin, OH: OCLC, 2003, V. 1, pp. viii-ix.
4. Taylor, Arlene G., Introduction to Cataloguing and Classification 10th ed., Chapter 15, Decimal Classification, mss, 2005, pp. 5-6.
5. Dewey Decimal Classification and Relative Index: /devised by Melvil Dewey. 22nd/edited by John s. Mitchell et al., Dublin, OH: OCLC, 2003, V. 1, pp. l-lviii.
6. *Ibid.*, pp. xix-xx.
7. Dewey Decimal Classification: ACOC Seminar, Sydney, July 2003.
8. Mortimer, Mary, Learn DDC 22, USA: Total Recall Publications Inc., 2007, p. 106.

# 2

# How to Classify a Work with DDC

**What is Classification:** Classification is a logical system for the arrangement of knowledge. A grouping together of like objects.

Prior to Melvil Dewey, library books were shelved in a fixed location on a particular shelf. Dewey developed his system of relative location between 1873 and 1876.

The principle given by him is that the books are numbered according to their intellectual content. This system allows more flexibility with locations.

**Notation:** In DDC, the notation is expressed in Arabic numerals. All classification numbers contain at last three digits. Where more than three digits needed, a decimal point follows the third digit.

**Main parts of DDC:** Introduction, Glossary, Manual, Tables, Main Classes, Schedules (V2-V3) and Relative Index are the main parts of DDC. DDC is a hierarchical classification proceeding from general to more specific in terms of discipline. The universe of knowledge is divided into ten main classes. These ten classes are further divided in ten divisions represented by second digit and each division has ten sections represented by third digit. Structural hierarchy means that all the topics are part of all the broader topics. The hierarchical structure is continued and incorporated in the notation which is lengthened by one digit for each more specific subject, e.g.

600 – Technology

640 – Home and family management

646 – Sewing clothing, management of personal and family life
646.7 – Management of personal and family life
646.72 – Care of hair, face, skin, nails
646.724 – Care of hair
646.724 8 – Wigs

The structural hierarchy means that all the topics, except for the ten main classes, are subordinate to and part of the broader topics above them, e.g.

500 – Natural sciences and mathematics
520 – Astronomy and allied sciences
523 – Specific classical bodies and phenomena
523.4 – Peanuts, asteroids and other subject
523.43 – Mars

The same subject may appear in a number of disciplines. Clothes as a subject can be found in three different classes.

391 – Costumes
646 – Home economics and Sewing
687 – Commercial manufacture
746.92 – Arts and fashion design

**Interdisciplinary number:** An interdisciplinary number is a number used for works covering a subject from the perceptions of more than one discipline. It is often identified by a class here interdisciplinary works. The interdisciplinary number for a subject always appears first next to that subject in relative index. For example, clothing has several different Dewey numbers depending on the discipline."[1]

## Classifying with DDC

Classifying with the DDC requires determination of the subject, the disciplinary focus and if applicable, the approach or form. All knowledge is divided into ten main classes which are listed below.

The classifier should study and go through the ten main classes, each main class is divided into 100 divisions and each division is divided in 1000 sections.

000 = Computer science, information, general works
100 = Philosophy, Parapsychology
200 = Religion
300 = Social Sciences
400 = Languages
500 = Natural Sciences and Mathematics
600 = Technology (Applied Sciences)
700 = the Arts Fine and Decorative Arts
800 = Literature (Bells-letters) and rhetoric
900 = History, Geography and Auxiliary Disciplines.[2]

The classifier should not fail to look through the six tables in Vol. I (DDC). He should also observe carefully the special nature of main class 800 (Literature) and 000. In Literature, subjects disregarded for work of literature. Arrangement of individual workers is first by discipline literature, then by original language, then by literary form, then by period of composition. Detailed instructions, tables and examples are given in (vol. 1).

In main class (000), general encyclopedic works (030), general serial publication (050), general newspapers (071-079), general collections (080) and general publications of general organizations (061-068) have no specific subject and are part of one discipline. The most significant thing about them after their generality is their form. Arrangement of these generality is first by form, then by language or place as the schedules period.

There are four important steps to classify a work. There are four steps before assigning the class number to a work.

1. Determine the subject of the work
2. Select the appropriate discipline
3. Find the most specific number for the subject
4. Add to the number using DDC's number building features.

**1. Determining the subject of a work:** We determine the subject of a work from the title. But sometimes we need to analysis the table of contents, index, and chapter headings, introduction of the book, preface. The book jacket contains a summary of the subject content. Sometimes subject experts (teachers) may be required to determine the subjects of the work.

**2. Determining the discipline of a work:** A work is classed in the discipline or field of study for which the work is intended rather than the discipline from which the work derives. This enables the works that are used together to be found together, e.g. a general work by a zoologist on a agriculture pest control should be classed in agriculture not in zoology along with other works on agriculture pest control[2] [Xliiip, [5.4] of tables (V. 1)].

**Number building:** There are four sources of notation for building precise number for a work

(A) The Table 1 standard sub-divisions

(B) Tables 2-6

(C) Other parts of the schedules

(D) Add tables in the schedules.

After determining the subject and discipline of the work, there are two basic approaches to classification:

1. Direct through the schedules
2. Indirect through the index.

**The relative index:** For many subjects, different aspects are located in different classes. The relative index brings together (relates) the different aspects located in different classes in which they are to be found. No (one) class can cover all aspects of a subject. If the term is not found in the index, we should try a broader term, or consult the schedule and tables directly. The numbers found from the index should be confirmed from the schedules. Never rely on Index alone.

*Beginners will usually find the second approach.* But it is not recommended because it delays the process of becoming acquainted with the system. A classifier should note that whether he is a beginner or an expert, he should never class solely from the index.

At each step the classifier should look carefully at the notes and directions, making certain that he has not followed a false track, e.g.

Dogs.

At first go to the index. In index under dogs we will see following numbers.

Dogs – 636.7

Animal husbandry – 636.7

Predator control technology – 636.083 9

Zoology – 599.772

Then go to schedule and see this number 636.7. This is a suitable number. In order to make it certain then go to 599.772. You will see this number is science oriented. You can also check 636.083 9 for certainty. This number 636.7 suits for the work dogs.

**Direct from schedules:** There are three summaries in DDC. After determine the subject of a work select a suitable class out of ten main classes. Then from second summary select one of the suitable divisions out of the ten divisions of that main class. Then from the third summary select a suitable section of that division. When you find three digits or base number, follow instructions if there are any in the schedule or add standard subdivisions to the base number. If there are more facets in the title then follow the preference and citation order (see in next pages).

**More than one subject in the same discipline:** A work may cover multiple aspects of one subject or more than one subject in a discipline.

The following guidelines are suggested:

Class a work dealing with interdicted subjects with that subject is being acted upon. For example, class an analytical work dealing with Shakespeare's, influence on Keats with Keats.

Class a work on two subjects with the subject receiving fuller treatment.

**First of two rules:** If two subjects receive equal treatment and are not used to introduce or explain one another. Class the work with the subject whose number comes first in the DDC schedules. For example, a history dealing equally with United States and Japan in which United States is discussed first and is given first in the title is classed with the history of Japan because 952 Japan precedes 973 United States.

But sometimes, specific instructions are given to use numbers that do not come first in schedules. For example, at 598, the note "class comprehensive works on worm-blooded vertebrates in 599" tells the classifier to ignore the first of two rules and class a work on "birds (598) and mammals (599)" in 599 which is comprehensive number for worm-blooded vertebrates.

Also disregard the first of two rules when the two topics are the two major subdivisions of a subject. For example, effects of heat on gases and solids, number for effects of heat on gases (536.412) and effect of heat on solids (536.44). Works covering both of these topics are classed in 536.41 not 536.412.

**The rule of three:** Class a work on three or more subjects that are all subdivisions of a broader subject in the first higher number that includes them all (unless one subject is treated more fully than the others). For example, a history of Portugal (946.9), Sweden (948.5) and Greece (949.5) is classed with the history of Europe (940).[3]

Whenever you get stuck it is always good idea to look to see a note in manual. Following example,

"Works about Donkeys as animals will go with works about other animals in zoology discipline – DDC division 590.

A book of folk tales about Donkeys will go with other books of folk tales in the folklore discipline – DDC division 390.

The subject of domesticated or working Donkeys is classed alongside other domesticated animals, in agriculture discipline DDC division 630.

A book of paintings & sculpture of Donkeys will go with other art books in the arts discipline – DDC class 700."

Always remember DDC is organized by disciplines or field of study not by subjects. When thinking of disciplines, remember that a discipline is a field of study—something that can be taught. For example, Horticulture can be taught, so it is a discipline, where as strawberries cannot be taught, so they are subject.[4]

**Table of last resort:** When several numbers have been found for the work in hand and each seems as good as the next. The following table of resort (in order of preference) may be used as a guideline in the absence of any other rule:

Table of last resort

1. Kinds of things
2. Parts of things
3. Materials from which things, kinds or parts are made
4. Properties of things, kinds, parts or materials
5. Processes within things, kinds, parts or materials
6. Operations upon things, kinds, parts or materials
7. Instrumentalities for performing such operations.

For example, Surveillance by Border Patrols could be classed in either 363.285 Border Patrol or 363.232 Patrol & Surveillance are processes performed by Police services.

Do not apply this table or any other guideline if appears to disregard the author's intention and emphasis.[5]

### Citation and Preference Order

Citation order must be considered when multiple aspects or characteristics of a subject (such as age, area, gender, historical periods, and national origin) are provided for in the classification and single work treats more than one of them.

Citation order allows the classifier to build a number using two or more facets (characteristics) as specified in instruction notes. A classifier can determine from the instruction given in the schedule, the sequence in which the facets will be ordered. For example, world history of Jews in 18th century.

909.04 – History with respect to ethnic and national groups

Add to base number 909.04 notation 05-9 from Table 5

924 – Jews (T5)

909.04 + 924

909.049 24 then add 0 and to the result add the numbers following 909 in 909.1 – 909.8

18th century = 909.7 (Inner Table, p. 835, V. 3)

909.04924 + 0 + ~~909~~.7

909.049 240 7

This note gives the following citation order for the individual facets of the full subjects.

World history + specific ethnic or national group + historical period.

The historical period is introduced by the facet indicator zero (0).

**Preference Order:** When there are number of characteristics and aspects are given in a title but there is no provision to show more than one of the aspects, then it is a matter of preference. An example of preference instruction is found at 305.9.

305.9 – Occupational & miscellaneous groups

Unless other instructions are given, class a subject with aspects in two or more subdivisions of 305.9 in number coming last. Unemployed Librarians = 305.909 2 not 305.906 94 in the DDC hierarchy.[6]

Citation Liv – Lviip., DDC, V. 1 Tables

305.909 – Generalists

Add to base number 305.909 the numbers following 0 in 001-099, e.g. (Librarians) 305.909 2. *The numbers following 0 in 001-099 replace the numbers following 09 in notation 0901-097 from Table 7 with the result that some numbers have been reused with new meanings.* As Table 7 has removed from DDC, 22nd Ed.

[p. 340, of schedule (000-599), V. 2, 2003 of DDC]

Librarians = 305.909 + θ20 = 305.9092

In this title first 0 in 020 is replaced by 09

Computer Programmers = 305.909 + 0051 = 305.909 051

In this title 0 in 0051 is replaced by 09

305.91-99

Add to base numbers 305.9 notation 100-999, e.g. agricultural occupations in general 305.963

305.9 + 630

305.963

Notation 100-999 replaces notation 1-9 from Table 7 with the result that many numbers have been reused with new meanings.[7]

## References


1. www.Oclc/.org/dewey/versions/print/intro.pdf, viewed on 5 August 2016.
2. Dewey Decimal Classification and Relative Index: /devised by Melvil Dewey. 22nd/edited by John s. Mitchell et al., Dublin, OH: OCLC, V. 1, pp. xli-xliii
3. *Ibid.*, pp. xliv-xlv.
4. Web Dewey.
5. Kaushik, S.K. *DDC 22nd—A Practical Approach*. New Delhi: Ess Ess, 2004, p. 9.
6. Dewey Decimal Classification and Relative Index: /devised by Melvil Dewey-22nd /edited by John S. Mitchell et al., Dublin, OH: OCLC, V. 1, pp. liv-lvii.
7. Dewey, Melvil, DDC22/edited by John S. Mitchell, V. 2 (000-599) Ohio: OCLC, 2003, pp. 340-41.

# 3
# Glossary

**Glossary:** In simple words, glossary means a list of often difficult or specialized words with their definitions, often placed at the back of a book. In DDC, the glossary defines terms used in the introduction and throughout the schedules, tables and manual. Fuller explanations and examples for many terms may be found in the relevant sections of the introduction.

**Abridged Edition:** A shortened version of the Dewey Decimal Classification system that is a logical truncation of the notational and structural hierarchy of corresponding full edition on which it is based, the abridged edition is intended for general collection of 20000 titles or less.

**Area Table:** Table 2 gives notation for geographic areas. Areas of the world are listed systematically not alphabetically. Area table notation may be used with other numbers in the schedules and tables.

**Artificial Digit:** A letter or other symbol used optionally as a substitute for digits 0-9 to provide a more prominent location or shorter notation for a language, literature, religion, ethnic or national group, etc. There are options in DDC. In order to give local emphasis and make the notation small we can use alphabets in some places. For example, there are number of options in DDC, e.g. Punjabi **Literature** = 891.42. We can use 8P in order to make the notation small for Punjabi **Language** = 491.42 we can use 4P. Such kind of option B is given on page 896 of volume 1 of DDC.

**Author Number means Book Number:** Book number: A library using the Cutter-Sanborn system can have D548D indicates David Copperfield by Dickenson where D stands for Dickens, 548 stands for "ickens" and D stands for David Copperfield.

**Broad Classification:** The classification of works in broad categories by logical abridgement, even when more specific no-one available, e.g. the use of 641.5 = cooking instead of 641.597 2 Mexican Cooking for a cook book of Mexican recipes. Broad classification is the opposite of close classification.

**Call Number:** Call number consists of book number and class number and other data such as date, volume no, copy number and location symbol. It is a set of letters, numbers, and other symbols (in combination or alone).

**Centered Entry:** An entry representing a subject covered by a span of numbers, e.g. 372-374 specific levels of education. The entry called centered because the span of numbers appears in the center of the page in the print version of the DDC rather than in the number column on the left side of the page. Centered entries are identified by the symbol > in the number column.

**Class-here Note:** A note that identifies topics that are equivalent to the whole of the class under which the note appears. The topic as a whole is classed in the number under which the note appears, parts of the topic are classed in the most appropriate subdivision of the number. Topics identified in class here notes, even if broader or narrower than the heading, are said to approximate the whole of the number, therefore S.S. may be added for topics in class-here notes also may identify the comprehensive or interdisciplinary number for a subject.

**Class Number:** Notation that designates the class to which a given item belongs.

**Classification:** Classification is a logical system for the arrangement of knowledge.

**Classify:** To arrange a collection of items according to the notational order of a classification systems.

**Cutter Numbers:** The notation in a book number derived from the cutter three-figure Author Table, the Cutter-Sanborn three-figure Author Table or the OCLC four-figure cutter tables. The OCLC four-figure cutter tables are revised and expanded versions of the cutter three-figure. Author table and the Cutter-Sanborn three-figure author tables.

**DDC Summaries:** A listing of the first three levels (main classes, divisions and sections) of the Dewey decimal classification system. The headings associated with the numbers in the summaries have been edited for browsing purposes and may not match the complete headings found.

**Facet Indicator:** A digit used to introduce notation representing a characteristic of the subject. For example, 0 is often used as a facet indicator to introduce standard subdivision concepts.

**First of Two Rule:** The rule instructing that works dealing equally with two subjects that are not used to introduce or explain one another are classed in the number coming first in the schedules or tables.

**Relocation:** The shifting of a topic from one number to another number that differs from the old number in respects other than length. Notes at both ends of the relocation identify the new and former numbers."[1]

## Reference

1. Dewey Decimal Classification and Relative Index/devised by Melvil Dewey: 22nd ed./edited by John S. Mitchell, et al., Dublin: OCLC, 2003, 1-4V, V. 1, pp. lxv-lxxiv.

# 4

# Use of Standard Subdivisions SS (Table 1)

There are six tables in DDC 22nd edition. First table is called standard subdivisions. It can be used with any number from schedule. Rules for adding SS to a class number have been given in Volume 1 of D.D.C. (pp. lii-liv) and instructions for the use of SS are given in manual on (pp. 5-19 in V. 1).

1. We can use SS to any number in the schedule without any instruction given in schedule. For example,

Journal of Labor Economics = 331.05

Formulas in Chemistry = 540.212

In the above class numbers Labor Economics and Chemistry are the subjects and Journal and Formulas are SS, respectively from Table 1. There is no instruction to use SS in the schedule under these numbers. There is not instruction to add SS in Schedule; even then SS from Table 1 are to be added to above Numbers 331 and 540.

2. Standard subdivisions are not to be used if standard subdivision type class is already enumerated in the schedule. For example,

503 Dictionary of Science

401 Philosophy and Theory of Language

3. All the Standard Subdivisions start with 0 (Zero). It means zero is a normal connecting symbol for SS Notation.

SS generally consists of two or more digits of, in which the first is zero and may be used with any number at any level whenever these are appropriate. But in some cases, for various reasons, notation beginning with 0 is or has previously been used for another purpose, in such cases the classifier is instructed to use two zeros or three zeros or even four zeros. In 22nd edition, use of SS with two zeros, three zeros and four zeros is given in the summary in the beginning of each main class. For example, Encyclopedia of Feudalism = 321.3 + 003.

Under summary of 321 systems of government and states, there is instruction

Summary

321.001-.009 Standard Subdivisions

It means we will use SS with all numbers of from 321.00-321.99 with two zeros instead of one.

### Adding Standard Subdivisions from Table 1

(1) SS represents a recurring physical form (such as dictionary, periodical, or index) or (approach such as history or research) and thus is applicable to any subject or discipline that covers or approximates the whole of the meaning of the number. There are few examples with SS concept underlined (in some cases an extra 0 precedes the SS according to instructions found in the schedules):

| | | |
|---|---|---|
| 150.5 | = | Periodical of Psychology |
| 230.003 | = | Dictionary of Christianity |
| 340.025 73 | = | Directory of Lawyers in the U.S. |
| 401 | = | Philosophy of Language |
| 507.8 | = | Use of apparatus and equipment in the study & teaching of science, e.g. Science Fair Projects |
| 624.028 5 | = | Computer applications in civil engineering |
| 796.912 092 | = | Biography of a figure skater |
| 808.007 1 | = | Teaching of rhetoric |

(2) Notation from Table 1 (SS) may be added to any number in the schedules unless there is a specific instruction to the contrary. The classifier should not use more than one zero unless instructed

to do so. If more than one zero is needed, the number of zeros is always indicated in the schedule.

When using SS with numbers built by adding from Tables 2-6 or other parts of the schedule, be sure to check the table or schedule used for segment preceding the SS for special information's on the number of zeros.

(3) Do not add multiple standard subdivisions to the same number except when specifically instructed to do so.

(4) When standard subdivisions are displaced to non-zero numbers usually for geographic treatment, the full range of SS may be added, e.g. the management of panel institutions in Great Britain 365.941 068.

(5) SS should not be used where redundant, where the subdivision means the same as the base number.

(6) The table of preference at the beginning of the table 1 yields two other rules, the rule of application and the rule of zero. By the rule of application, teaching financial management in Hospital administration is classed in 362.110 681 not 632.110 71, even though notation 07 is above notation 068 in the table of preference. The rule of zero over rides the table of preference when SS are displaced to non zero positions e.g. management of prisons in Great Britain 365.941 068 not 365.068. The most important rule with respect to standard sub divisions is that they are added only for works that cover the whole of the subject of the number or approximate the whole of the subject of the number. For e.g. A work on black widow spiders in California & there is not a specific number for spiders 595.44 not 595.440 979 4, the number for spiders in California. The classifier should not specify California because black widow spiders do not approximate the whole universe of spiders in California.[1]

## Reference

1. Dewey Decimal Classification and Relative Index: /devised by Melvil Dewey. 22nd /edited by John S. Mitchell et al., Dublin, OH: OCLC, V. 1, pp. lii-liv.

(1) **Formulas in Chemistry**
540 = Chemistry
–0212(T1) = Formulas (T1)
54θ + 0212
540.212

(2) **Correspondence Courses in Public Administration**
351 = Public Administration
–0715 = Correspondence Courses
351 + 0715
351.071 5

(3) **International Organizations in Trade**
381 = Trade
–0601 = International organizations (T1)
381 + 0601
381.060 1

(4) **Serial Publications in Astronomy**
520 – Astronomy
–05 = Serial Publications (T1)
52θ + 05
520.5

(5) **History of Philosophy**
100 = Philosophy
–09 = History (T1)
1θθ + 09 (as these are filler zeros) Never cut zeros of standard sub divisions
109

(6) **A Journal of Hinduism**
Hinduism = 294.5
–05 = Journal (T1)
294.5 + 05
294.505

(7) **Directories of Musicians**
780 = Musicians
–025 = Directory (T1)
78θ + 025
780.25

(8) **Dictionary of Sciences**
500 = Sciences
–03 = Dictionary (T1)
5~~00~~ + 03
503.03

(9) **History of Medicines**
Medicines = 610
–09 = History (T1)
61~~0~~ + 09
610.9

(10) **Research in Mammals**
599 = Mammals
–072 = Research (T1)
599 + 072
599.072

(11) **Encyclopedia of Textile**
646 = Textile
–03 = Encyclopedia (T1)
646 + 03
646.03

**Use of Two Zeros in SS**

(12) **Market research in silk textiles**
Silk textiles = 677.39
Instruction: (677.001 – .009)
–0688 = Market Research (T1)
677.39 + 00688
677.390 068 8

(13) **Dictionary of Diseases**
616 = Diseases
03 = Dictionary
616.001 – .003 Standard Subdivisions
616 + 003
616.003

(14) **A Dictionary of Algebra**
512 = Algebra
Instruction: (512.001 – .009)

03 = Dictionary (T1)
512 + 003
512.003

(15) **Study and Teaching of Library Classification**
025.42 = Classification and shelf listing
025.001 – .009 standard subdivisions
–007(T1) = Study and teaching instead of –07
025.42 + 007
025.420 07

(16) **Encyclopedia of Constitutional Law**
342 = Constitutional Law
(Use 342.001 – 342.009 for SS)
03 = Encyclopedia (T1)
342 + 003
342.003

(17) **Journal of Human Anatomy**
611 = Human Anatomy
(611.001 – 611.009 for SS)
05 = Journal (T1)
611 + 005
611.005

(18) **Patent of Refrigerator**
621.57 = Refrigerator
621.400 1 – .400 9 Standard Subdivisions
–0272 = Patents (T1)
621.57 + 00272
621.570 027 2

(19) **Research on Colon Classification**
025.435 = Colon Classification
–072= Research (T1)
025.001 – .009 Standard Subdivisions
025.435 + 0072
025.435 007 2

(20) **Research on Heart Surgery**
617.412 = Heart Surgery
–072 = Research
617.412 + 072
617.412 072

## Use of Three Zeros

(21) **Organizations of Libraries**
026 = Libraries, Archives, Information Centers devoted to specific subjects and disciplines
Instruction: 0001 –.0005 Standard Subdivisions
–06 = Organizations and Management (T1)
026 + 0006
026.000 6

(22) **Central Europe during Middle Ages**
Central Europe = 943
.0001 – .0008 = Standard Subdivisions
.000901 – 000905 = Historical Periods
Add to base 943.00090 the numbers following –090 in notation 0901 – 0905 from Table 1.
–0902 = Middle Ages (T1)
943.00090 + ~~090~~2
943.000 902

(23) **Audio video Treatment of Central Europe**
Central Europe = 943
.0001 – .0008 = Standard Subdivisions
–028 = Audio video Treatment (T1)
943 + 00028
943.000 28

(24) **Journal of Pediatrics**
Pediatrics = 618.92
0920 001 – .920 007 = Standard Subdivisions
–05 = Journal (T1)
618.92 + 0005
618.920 005

(25) **Theory of Economics Services**
Economics Services = 338.47
338.47 Instruction
.470001 – .470009 Standard Subdivisions for Services
–01 = Philosophy and Theory (T1)
338.47 + 0001
338.470 001

(26) **Theory of Service Tax**
Service Tax = 336.278
Instruction:
.2780001 – .278.0009 = Standard Subdivisions
–01 = Theory and Philosophy (Table 1)
336.278 + 0001
336.278 000 1

(27) **Cases of Insurance Law**
Insurance Law = 346.086
Instruction:
.0860001 – .0860009 = Standard Subdivisions
Notation from Table 1 as modified under 342–346
0264 = Cases (inner table in Schedule under 342–347)
346.086 + 000264
346.086 000 264

(28) **Mathematics for Engineers**
510 = Mathematics
–024 = the subject for persons in specific occupations (T1)
620 = Engineers
51~~0~~ + 024 + 62
510.246 2

(29) **Astrology for Social Scientists**
Astrology = 133.5
–024 = the subject for persons in specific occupations (T1)
300 = Social Sciences
133.5 + 024 + 300
133.502 43

(30) **Reference Service among Lawyers**
025.52 = Reference + Information Service
088 = Occupational and Religious Groups
340 = Law
So 025.52 + 088 +34~~0~~
025.520 883 4

(31) **Reference and Information Services among Managers**
Reference and Information Services = 025.52
–088 = Occupational Religious Groups (T1)

658 = Managers
025.52 + 088 + 658
025.520 886 58

(32) **Cooperative Information Services = 025.523**
–088 = Occupational Religious Groups (T1)
–088 001 – 088 999 = Specific Occupational Religious Groups (T1)
297 = Muslims (Religious Group)
025.523 + 088297
025.523 088 297

(33) **Cooperative Information Services among Sikhs**
025.523 + 088 + 294.6
025.523 088 294 6

(34) **Psychology for Managers**
Psychology = 150
–024 = the subject for persons in specific occupations (T1)
658 = Managers
15θ + 024 + 658
150.246 58

(35) **Wedding and Marriage Customs among Punjabis**
392.5 = Wedding and Marriage Customs
–089 = Ethnic and National Group
–9142 = Punjabis
392.5 + 089 + 9142
392.508 991 42

(36) **Teachers of Indian Origin in U.K.**
371.1 = Teachers
–089 = Ethnic and National Groups (T1)
Class here Ethnic and National Minorities
–91411 = Indians (T5)
371.1 + 089 + 91411
371.108 991 411

## Table of Preference

Unless there are specific instructions, it is recommended that when the classifier finds that two or more standard subdivisions are applicable to a particular work, he should use the table of precedence to determine which one he should use. If for some reason, he feels he must use more than one, that table indicates the order in which to use them.

In the beginning of Standard Subdivisions, the following table of preference is given, e.g., Language and Communication in Education and Research –07 (not –014);

| | |
|---|---|
| Special Topics = | –04 |
| Persons = | –092 |
| Auxiliary techniques and procedures: apparatus, equipment, materials | –028 |
| Education research related topics | –07 |
| (Except –074, –075) | |
| Management | –068 |
| Philosophy and theory | –01 |
| The subject as a profession, occupation, hobby | –023 |
| The subject for persons in specific occupation | –024 |
| Directories of persons and organizations | –025 |
| Patents and identification marks | –027 |
| Commercial Miscellany | –029 |
| Organizations | –0601-0609 |
| Organizations (with subdivisions) | –06 |
| History and description with respect to kinds of persons | –08 |
| Treatment by specific continents, countries, localities: extraterrestrial worlds | –093-099 |
| Treatment by areas, reasons, places in general | –091 |
| Maintenance and repair | –0288 |
| Historical periods | –0901-0905 |
| Forecasting and forecasts | –0112 |
| Museums, collections, exhibits | –074 |
| Museum activities and services collecting | –075 |
| Review and exercise | –076 |

| | |
|---|---|
| Programmed texts | –077 |
| Illustrations, models, miniatures | –022 |
| Tabulated and related materials | –021 |
| Synopsis and outlines | –0202 |
| Humorous treatment | –0207 |
| Audio visual treatment | –0208 |
| Language and communication | –014 |
| Dictionaries, encyclopedia, concordances | –03 |
| Historical and geographic treatment (without subdivision) | –09 |
| Serial publications | –05 |

(37) **History of Teaching Economics at University Level**
Economics = 330
History = –09(T1)
Teaching = –07(T1)
Teaching at University Level = –0711 (T1)
63θ + 0711
630.711

In above title –07 have given preference over –09 according to Table of Preference. Similarly

(38) **Periodical on Research in Mathematics**
Mathematics = 510
Research = 072 (T1)
Periodical = –05 (T1)
51θ + 072
510.72

(39) **Encyclopedia of Research on Botany**
Botany = 580
Encyclopedia = –03
Research = 072
58θ + 072
580.72

(40) **History of Library Science at University Level in India**
Library Science = 020
History = 09

Teaching at University Level (Higher Level) = –0711
Instruction: Add to Base Number 0711 Notation 1–9 From Table 2.
02θ + 0711 + 54
020.711 54

(41) **Study of Celestial Mechanics in 19th Century**
Celestial Mechanics = 521
Study = –071 (T1)
19th Century = 09034 (T1)
521 + 071
521.071

**07 has preference over 09 in the above Preference Table**

(42) **Museum of Sikhs in 18th Century**
Sikhism = 294.6
Museum = –074
18th Century = –09031
294.6 + 074
294.607 4

(43) **Collection of Paintings in 17th Century**
Paintings = 750
Collections = –074 (T1)
17th Century = 09032 (T1)
75θ + 074
750.74

# 5

# Use of Geographic Areas, Historical Periods, Persons (Table 2)

This table lists the notations for geographical areas, historical periods and persons, and explains the organization of Table 2 for the procedure of adding subdivisions. The major use of Table 2 is with notation 09 from Table 1, where it can be added to every number in the schedule unless there are specific instructions to the contrary, e.g. reading instructions in primary schools of Australia 372.4 + 09 (SS) + 94 (T2). Sometimes area notation is added directly to the schedule number but only when specified in a note. Area table is also used through Standard Subdivisions like (023, 025, 029, 0272, 074, 079).

The use of two area numbers simultaneously are also used by connecting digit 0. Table 2 is also used through T5 and T6.

### (A) Use of Area through 09

When instruction is not given to add area directly in schedule but the title of the book demands area number. In such a case, we can add area number by SS 09 for historical, Geographical Persons treatment. We can also find instructions for the use of 09 (SS). Under –091, –092 and –093-999 in Table 1.

091-treatment by Area, regions, places in general

Add to base number 091 the numbers following –1 in notation –11-19 from Table 2, e.g. Torrid zone –0913; then add further as instructed under 093-099, e.g.

Conservation and preservation in tropical areas 0913028. Go to –093-099 (p. 212, V. 1).

This shows that 09 can be used as connecting symbol where instruction is not given to add area.

–093-099 under this 028-conservation and preservation (T1, p. 214).

So 0913 + 028 = 0913028

Under –0922 (T1, p. 213 of tables)

Add to base number 0922 notation 3-9 from Table 2

Rules for the use of 09 are also there in *Manual Tables* (pp. 13-14).

"The History of Rail Roads = 385.09 (not 385.090 3) but the history of railroads in the 19th century = 385.090 34. If in doubt do not use periods.

Do not use most recent period subdivision for works on current practice or the state-of-the-art of a subject, since most users will expect to find these works in the base number. However, use the latest period number when the nature of the subject requires attention to the changing situation, e.g. 320.905 11 for world political conditions in 2000-2009.

Use earlier historical periods only for retrospective works, not for contemporary works. For example, use 781.090 32 for a current work on music theory of the baroque, but use 781 for a reprint of a treatise on music theory written in 1620 (when baroque music was in style) p. 14 of *Manual Tables of DDC*, 22nd Ed.).

Use T1-09 for either or both aspects where the distinction is not made between the subject and the discipline (p. 13 of Table)

**National Groups**

French Desserts = 641.860 944 not 641.860 894 1

Use T1-09 not T1-089 to identity, distinguishing characters of a subject in an area where a specific group of people lives, e.g. Arab Architecture = 720.899 27

**(A) Major use of Table 2 through SS 09 From T1**

(1) **British Colonies in West Africa**
325.3 = Colonization
325.33-39 = Colonization by specific countries
Add to base number 325.3 notation 3-9 from Table 2, e.g. Colonization by United Kingdom = 325.341; Colonization by United Kingdom in West Africa = 325.341 096 6
41 = United Kingdom
09 = T1 (SS)
66 = West Africa
Explanation of the number.
325.3 + 41 + 09 + 66
325.341 096 6
This title show 09 is used to connect two areas.

(2) **Standard of Living in Rural Areas**
339.47= Standard of living
09 = Connecting digit (from SS T1)
1734 = Rural Regions (T2)
So 339.47 + 09 + 1734
339.470 917 34

(3) **Emigration from Japan to United States**
Emigration = 325.2
325.23-29 = Emigration from specific continents, countries, Locality
Add to base number 325.2 Notation 3-9 from Table 2, e.g. Emigration from Japan 325.252 (p. 389, V. 2)
52 = Japan (T2)
73 = United States (T2)
09 = connecting symbol from SS
325.2 + 52 + 09 + 73
325.252 097 3

(4) **Child Labor in India**
Child Labor = 331.31
No Instruction is given to add areas Notation. So
–09 = (T1) (SS)
–54 = India (T2)

331.31 + 09 + 54
331.310 954

(5) **Freedom of Press in Developing Countries**
Freedom of Press = 323.445
–09 = SS (T1)
–1724 = Developing Countries. So
323.445 + 09 + 1724
323.445 091 724

(6) **Freedom of Conscience and Religion in Pakistan**
Freedom of conscience and religion = 323.442
No instruction for adding area
–09 = T1 (SS)
Pakistan= –5491
323.442 + 09 + 5491
323.442 095 491

(7) **Property Rights in Communist Countries**
Property Rights = 323.46
No instruction to add area so
–09 = T1 = SS
–1717 = Communist Block
323.46 + 09 + 1717
323.460 917 17

(8) **Freedom of Speech in Non-Aligned Countries**
Freedom of Speech = 323.443
–09 = SS (T1)
–1716 = Non-Aligned Countries
323.443 + 09 + 1716
323.443 091 716

(9) **Right of Petition in Developed Countries**
Right of Petition = 323.48
No instruction for area
–09 = SS (T1)
–1724 = Developing Countries (T2)
323.48 + 09 + 1724
323.480 917 24

(10) **Freedom of Press in Urban Areas**
323.445 = Freedom of Press

–09 = SS (T1)
–1732 = Urban Areas
323.445 + 09 + 1732
323.445 091 732

(11) **Treatment of Rectum and Anus in Children in India**
618.92 = Children
Under 618.921-929
Add to base number 618.92 the numbers following 616 in notation 616.1-616.9
Under
616.35 = *Diseases of Rectum and Anus
As it is asterisk follow instructions under 616.1-616.9
(Under 616.1-616.9)
062–069
Add to 06 the numbers following 615.8 in 615.82–615.89
615.8422 = x-ray therapy
009 = Historical and Geographical Treatment
54 = India (Table 2)
618.92 + ~~616~~.35 + 06 + ~~615.8~~422 + 009 + 54
618.923 506 422 009 54

### (B) Direct Use of Table 2 with Schedule Number

There are sufficient instructions to use area Table 2 directly to the base number from schedule, e.g. Bibliographies of specific places like British National Bibliography.

(12) **British National Bibliography**
015 = Bibliographies and Catalogues of Works from Specific Places
41 = Britain (T2)
Instruction:
Add to base number 015 notation 1–9 from Table 2
015 + 41
015.41
Similarly

(13) **Indian National Bibliography = 015.54**
015 + 54 = 015.54

(14) **Journalism in India = 079.54**
079 = Journalism and newspapers in other geographic areas
Instruction: Add to base number 079 notation 1–9 from Table 2.
–54 = India
079 + 54 (T2)
079.54

(15) **Political Conditions in Egypt**
320.9 = Political Conditions
320.901-.99
Historical, Geographic, Persons Treatment
Add to base number 320.9 notation 01-9 from Table 2
Egypt = 62
320.9 + 62
320.962

(16) **Similarly Political Conditions in India** = 320.9 + 54 = 320.954

(17) **Political Conditions in Punjab**
320.9 = Political conditions
–54552 = Punjab
320.9 + 54552
320.954 552

(18) **Emigration from Japan**
Emigration = 325.2
Instruction: add to base number 325.2 notation 3-9 from Table 2
325.2 + 52
325.252

(19) **Economic Conditions of Iraq**
330.9 = Economic Conditions of a Specific Country
Instruction: add to base number 330.9 notation from 3-9 from Table 2.
Iraq = 567
330.9 + 567
330.956 7

(20) **National Library of India**
027.5 = National Library
027.53–59 Specific institutions
Add to base number 027.5 notation 3-9 from Table 2 for Area Served.
027.5 + 54 (T2) (India)
027.554

(21) **Political Parties in India**
Political Parties = 324.2
Under
324.24-29 parties in specific countries in the modern world
Instruction: Add Areas notation 4-9 to base number 324.2 from Table 2 for the specific country.
–54 = India
Class no. 324.2 + 54
324.254

(22) **Similarly Parties of France**
= 324.2 + 44 = 324.244 (e.g. in Schedule)
Parties in Specific Countries in the modern world (p. 377 of Schedule)

(23) **French Communist Party in Paris**
Parties of France = 324.2+44 then add to the number according to the table under 324.24-29, e.g. Parties of Paris = 324.244
075 = Communist Party (inner table under on pp. 377-78)
09 = SS
44361 = Paris
324.2 + 44 + 075
324.244 075

(24) **Similarly Communist Party of India**
324.2 + 54 + 075 (Communist Parties from schedule, p. 378)
324.254 075

(25) **Higher Education in Mexico**
Higher Education = 378

Instruction under 378.4-9 higher education in a specific country. Add to base number 378 notation 3-9 from Table 2 (p. 823, V. 2)
Mexico = 72
378 + 72
378.72

(26) **Management of Restaurants in Spain**
647.95 = eating and drinking places
Inst.: Add areas notation to base number 647.95 notation 3-9 from Table 2
46 = Spain (T2)
647.95 + 46
647.954 6

(27) **Public Education Policies in USA**
Education Policies = 379
Instruction under 379.4-9
Add to base number 379 notation 4-9 from Table 2
73 = USA (T2)
379 + 73
379.73

(28) **Cultural Exchange = 303.482**
303.4821-4829 Contact between specific areas
Add to base number 303.482 notation 1-9 from Table 2, e.g.
Cultural exchanges with China 303.482 + 51
303.482 51

(29) **Constitutional Law in India**
Constitutional Law = 342
Under 342.3-9 specific Jurisdiction
Instruction:
Add to base number 342 areas notation 3-9 from Table 2 to base number 342
342 + 54 (T2) (India)
342.54

(30) **Foreign Policy of India**
Foreign Policy = 327
Under 327.3-9
Add to base number 327 notation 3-9 from Table 2

India = –54(T2)
327 + 54
327.54

(31) **Economic Policy of UK**
337 = International Economics
337.3 – 9 Instruction
Add to base number 337 notation 3-9 from Table 2, e.g. For UK = 41(T2) policy of UK 337.41
337 + 41
337.41

(32) **Food Supply in Developing Countries**
338 = Production
Instruction
Add to base number 338.191 – the numbers following –1 in notation 11–19 from Table 2, e.g. food supply in developing countries 338.191 724
Important Note:
–1724 = developing regions
338.191 + ~~1~~724
338.191 724
Always omit the digits between "Following and In"

(33) **Food Supply in Developing Regions**
Food Supply = 338.191
Developing Regions = 1724
338.191 + ~~1~~724 (T2)
338.191 724

(34) **Food Supply in Urban Regions**
338.191 + ~~1~~732 (T2)
338.191 732

(35) **Economic Policies of United Kingdom**
338 = Production
338.93-99 Economic development and growth in specific continents, countries localities. Add to base number 338.9 notation 3-9 from Table 2, e.g. Economic Policies of United Kingdom 338.941
338.9 + 41

(36) **Subsidies in United Kingdom**
338 = Production
338.93-.99 = Economic development and growth in specific continents, countries and localities.
Instruction: add to base number 338.9 notation 3-9 from Table T2 and then add 0 to the result the numbers following 338.92 in 338.922-338.927
338.922 = Subsidies and grants
–41 = United Kingdom
338.9 + 41 + 0 + ~~338.92~~2
338.941 02

(37) **Postal Communication in Europe**
383 = Postal Communication
383.49- Historical, Geographical, Persons treatment of Postal Communications of Postal organizations and systems
Add to base number
383.49 Notation 1-9 from Table 2
–4 = Europe (T2)
383.49 + 4
383.494

(38) **Bird watching of East Africa**
Bird Watching= 598.072 34
598.072344-.072349
Instruction treatment of specific continents, countries, localities in modern world
Add to base number 598.07234 Notation 4-9 from Table 2
–676 = East Africa (T2)
598.07234 + 676
598.072 346 76

(39) **Similarly bird Watching in India**
598.07234 + 54(T2)
598.072 345 4

(40) **Adult Education in Canada**
374.9 = Adult Education
Instruction: Add to base no. 374.9 notation 1-9 from T2

–71 = Canada
374.9 + 71
374.971

### (C) Use of Two Numbers from Area Table 2 by Connecting-digit Zero

International relations between two countries: These relations may be of various kinds like foreign economic relations, foreign trade relations, and cultural relations. Sometimes two countries sign treaties and agreements of various kinds. How can we assign classification numbers to these titles? We should follow the instructions given in schedules and tables.

**Relation between Brazil and France 327.810 44**

International Relations = 327

Go to 327.3-9 foreign relations of specific continents and localities, foreign relations of specific countries.

Class-here Foreign Policy

Add to base number 327, notation 3-9 from Table 2. Relation between a nation and another country, add 0* and to the result add notation 1-9 from Table 2, e.g. Relation between Brazil and France 327.810 44. Between Brazil and Arab world 327.810 17 492 7.

(1) **International Relations between India and China**
327 = International Relations
327.3-9: Instruction as in the above number
–54 = India
0 = Connecting digit (CS)
–51 = China
327 + 54 (T2) + 0 (CS) + 51 (T2)
327.540 51

(2) **International Relations between India and Iran**
327 = International Relations
327.3-9: Instruction as in the above number
–54 (T2) = India
0 = Connecting digit for the areas (India and Japan)
–55 = Iran
327 + 54 + 0 + 55

327.540 55

You can add any areas first but we should prefer to use the areas first which is given at first place in the tables.

(3) **Foreign Economic Relations between India and USA**

337 = Foreign Economic Relations

Instruction: Add to base number 337 notation 3-9 from Table 2. Then for relation between that nation or region and another nation or region then add zero or to the result add notation 1-9 from Table 2.

–54 = India (T2)

0 = Connecting digit for two areas.

–73 = USA

337 + 54 + 0 + 73

337.540 73

(4) **Similarly Economic Relations between India and Italy**

337 + 54 + 0 + 45

337.540 45

(5) **Migration from USA to Australia**

Migration = 304.8

Instruction: Add to base number 304.8 notation 3-9 from Table 2 then add 0 and to the result add notation 1-9 from Table 2 for the origin. (p. 326 + 0.2)

–73 = USA

0 = Connecting digit

–94 = Australia

304.8 + 94 + 0 + 73

304.894 073

(6) **Migration from Punjab to USA**

Migration = 304.8

Instruction: Add to base number 304.8 notation 3-9 from Table 2 then for relation between that nation and region and another nation or region and then add 0 and to the result add notation 1-9 from Table 2 for the place of origin.

54 = India (T2)

Connecting Digit = 0

–73 = USA (T2)

–54552 = Punjab (T2)
304.8 + 54552 + 0 + 73
304.854 552 073

(7) **Similarly Migration from Punjab to UK**
304.8 + 41 + 0 + 54552
304.841 054 552

(8) **International Commerce of Areas, Regions Places in General**
382.091 = International Commerce of Areas, Regions Places in General e.g. International Commerce of Developing Countries
Add to the base No. 382.091 the numbers following –1 in notation – 11 – 19 from table 2.
382.09
–1724 = Developing Countries
382.09 + ~~1~~724
382.097 24

(9) **International Commerce between China and Japan (International Trade)**
382 = International Commerce
Instruction under 382.93-99
Add to base number 382.9 notation 3-9 from Table 2. Then add zero and again add notation 3-9 from Table 2 (p. 838, V. 2).
China = 51
Japan = 52
382.9 + 51 + 0 + 52
382.951 052

(10) **Trade between Canada and USA**
382.9 = Trade Agreements
382.9 + 71 + 0 + 73
382.971 073

(11) **Social Stratification of Indians to USA**
305.8 = Social stratification of Ethnic, National Groups
Add to base number 305.8 notation 05-9 from Table 5 (Social stratification of Chinese Australians = 305.8951094) (p. 337, V. 2).

–91411 (T5) = Indians
0 = Connecting digit to connect two areas.
–73 (T2) = United States
305.8 + 91411 + 0 + 73
305.891 411 073

(12) **Cultural Exchange between India and Russia**
303.482 = Cultural Exchange
Instruction: add to base number 303.482 notation 1-9 from Table 2 then add 0 and again add notation 1-9 from Table 2) (e.g. Cultural exchange between China and Japan = 303.482 510 52)
**Give priority in notation to the notation most affected.** If this cannot be determined give priority to the one coming first in Table 2, e.g. in United States class cultural exchange between United States and France 303.482 730 44 (p. 322, V. 2).
54 (T2) = India
0 = Connecting digit
47 = Russia
303.482 + 47 + 0 + 54
303.482 470 54

(13) **Atmospheric Pressure in the Mountains of Santa Cruz of California**
Atmospheric Pressure = 551.54
09 = Standard Subdivisions
Mountains = –143
–0 = Connecting digit
Santa Cruz = 79471 (California)
551.54 + 09 + 143 + 0 + 79471
551.540 914 307 947 1

(14) **US Educational Aid to Pakistan**
379.129 = Educational aid
Instruction: Add to base number 379.129 notation 1-9 from Table 2, then for area providing support, add 0 and again add notation 1-9 from Table 2 (e.g. French Educational aid to Asia= 379.1295044) (p. 825, V. 2).
Always follow the Instruction.

–73 = USA
0 = Connected digit
5491 = Pakistan
379.129 + 5491 + 0 + 73
379.129 730 549 1

(15) **Economic Policy of UK and France**
337 = International Economics
337.3-.9
Add to base number 337 notation 3-9 from Table 2
41 = UK (T2)
0 = Connecting digit
44 = France (T2)
337 + 41 + 0 + 44
337.410 44

(16) **Maps of Indian Forests**
912 = Maps
Forests = 152
0 = Connecting digit
–54 = India
912 + 152 + 0 + 54
912.152 054

**(D) Use of Table 2 through T1**

(1) **Research in Cosmetology in England**
646.72 = Cosmetology
–072 = Research (T1)
Add to base number –0720 notation 1-9 from Table 2
646.72 + 0720 + 42
646.720 720 42

(2) **Competitions in Football in California**
796.33 = Football
–079 = Competitions (T1)
Add to base number 079 notations 4-9 from Table 2
–794 = California
796.33 + 079 + 794
796.330 797 94

(3) **Commercial Miscellany of Milk Processing in India**
637.1 = Milk Processing

–029 = Commercial Miscellany (T1)
–0295 = Commercial Miscellany of Asia
–0295 = Add to base number 0295 the numbers following 5 in notation 51-59 from Table 2
–54 = India
637.1 + 0295 + 54
637.102 954

(4) **Law as a Profession in Great Britain**
340 = Law
–023 = the subject as a profession, occupation, hobby
Add to base number 023 notation following1-9 from Table 2
42 = England
340 + 023 + 42
340.234 2

(5) **Directories of Musicians of Ohio**
780.92 = Musician
–025 = Directories
Add to base number –025 notation 1-9 from Table 2
771 = Ohio
780.92 + 025 + 771
780.920 257 71

## (E) Use of T2 through Table T5

(1) **Social Status of Punjabis in USA**
305.8 = Ethnic and National Group
305.805-89 Specific ethnic and national groups
"Add to base number 305.8 notation 05-9 from Table 5, e.g. Comprehensive works on (Jews 305.892 4, Chinese 305.895 1, Chinese Australians 305.895 109 4 Inuit 305.867 12") (p. 337, V. 2)
–9142 = Punjabis (T5)
305.8 + 9142
0 = Connecting digit
–73 = USA (T2)
305.8 + 9142 + 0 + 73
305.891 420 73

(2) **Education of Eskimos in USA**
371.82 = Students
371.82 = Specific kind of students
371.821-829
Instruction: add to base number 371.82 the numbers following-08 in notation 081-089 from Table 1.
371.82 + ~~08~~9 (T1)
371.829-education of students of specific, ethnic or national origin 371.829
So base number = 371.829
Number for Eskimos = 97 + 971 (T6) = 971
[Instruction on p. 678, V. 1 under-97
Add to base number 97 the numbers following –97 in notation 971-979 from Table 6]
–971 = Eskimos (T5)
0 = Connecting digit
–73 = USA (T2)
371.829 + ~~97~~1 + 0 + 73
371.829 107 3

## (F) Use of Table 2 through T6

(1) **Coffee in Assamese Belt (People who Speak Assamese Language)**
Coffee = 633.73
Connecting digit = 09 (SS)
–175 (T2) Regions where specific language predominates (T2)
Instruction: Add to base number –175 notation 1-9 from Table 6.
Assamese Language = –91451 (T6)
Class number = 633.73 + 09 + 175 + 91451
633.730 917 591 451

(2) **Hospitality of People who Speak Orya**
395.3-Etiquette for Social occasions (Hospitality)
–09 (T1) = Connecting digit (SS)
–175 (T2) = Regions where specific languages predominate instruction: Add to base number –175 Notations 1-9 from Table 6.

–9145 (T6) = Orya
So 395.3 + 09 + 175 + 9145
395.309 175 914 5

(3) **Similarly Hospitality of Punjabis**
395.3 + 09 + 175 + 9142
395.309 175 914 2

(4) **Rescue Operations in the Regions where Muslims Predominate**
Rescue Operations = 629.458 5
–176 (T2) = Regions where specific religions predominate
–1762-1769 (T2) = other religions (because Muslim religion comes under other religions).
Instruction: Add to base number 176 the numbers following 29 in 292-299 (e.g. regions where Islam predominate-1767)
297-Islam (from schedule)
629.4585 + 09 + 176 + ~~29~~7
Class Number = 629.458 509 176 7

(5) **Interior Decoration and Artists in Islamic areas**
747 = Interior Decoration
–09 (T1) = SS
–176 (T2) = Religions where specific religion predominates
Under –1762-1769 = other religions
Add to base number -176 the number 29 in the number following 29 in 292-299.
297 = Islam (p. 289, V. 2)
Class number = 747 + 09 + 176 + ~~29~~7
Class Number = 747.091 767

(6) **Gambling in regions where Hindus Predominate**
364.172 = Gambling
–09 = SS (T1)
–176 (T2) = Regions where specific religion predominates
Under –1762-1769 = other religions
Hindus = 294.5 (from other religions)
Instruction: Add to base number –176 the number following 29 in 292-299.
So, class number 364.172 + 09 + 176 + ~~29~~4.5
364.172 091 764 5

(7) **Social Status of Women in Regions where Punjabi People Predominate**

305.42 = Social role and Status of Women
–09 (T1) = Connecting Digits
–174 (T2) = Regions where specific ethnic and national group predominates.
Instruction: Add to base number –174 notation 05-99 from Table 5.
–9142 (T5) = Punjabis
Class number = 305.42 + 09 + 174 + 9142
305.420 917 491 42

(8) **Similarly Social Role of Males in Regions where Punjabis Predominate**

305.31 + 09 + 174 + 9142 (T5)

From the above-mentioned examples we can come to know that we can use area Table 2 through Table 5 and Table 6 and through schedules.

–174 (Regions where specific ethnic and national group predominate) is divisible by Table 5.

–175 (Regions where specific languages predominate) is further divided by Table 6.

–176 (Regions where specific religions predominate) is further extended by religions taken from 29 and its subdivisions in the schedule.

In above titles three areas –174, –175, –176 are added to base numbers from schedules through –09 (SS) from Table 1.

# 6

# Use of Subdivisions for the Arts, for Individual Literatures, for Specific Literary Forms (Table 3)

### Number Building

Table 3 is never used alone, but may be used as required by add notes under subdivisions of individual literature or with base numbers for individual literatures identified by *(asterik) under 810-890. It is never used for works of or about such literatures end with the language notation. Table 3 is divided into three sub-tables, namely T3A, T3B and T3C.

Table 3A contains subdivisions for works by or about individual authors. Procedures for building numbers for individual authors.

### Rules (Steps)

(1) Look in the schedule 810-890 to find the base number for language. The base number may be identified in an add note, e.g. at 830.1 – 838 ("Add to base number 83") or another note under 891.4301-438, "Add to base number 891.43 (Hindi). After finding base number, find out if there is a specific literary form, if yes then go to step 2, if not go to instructions under-8 in Table 3A.

(2) In Table 3A, find the correct subdivision for the literary form, e.g. poetry-1, drama-2, fiction-3...and add this form with the base number, e.g. Hindi poetry 891.431. If the literary form appears as a subdivision of -8 miscellaneous writings go to the instructions under-8 in Table 3A, otherwise go to step 3.

(3) Turn back to the appropriate number in schedule 810-890 to see whether there is an applicable period table. If there is one, go to step 4, if not complete the class number by inserting a point between the 3rd and 4th digit, e.g. Khmer poetry by a 20th century author 895.932 1.

(4) Select the appropriate period number. Add this number to the number derived. Always insert a point after the third digit. The class number is complete.[1]

**Standard subdivisions are never added to individual authors.**

For example, Spenser's fairy queen 821.3.

(821 = English Poetry + 3 Elizabethan Period)" (p. 617, V. 1)

Three flow charts are given on (pp. 27, 31, 32, V. 1 of DDC 22nd) for

(1) Flow chart for works by or about an individual author.

(2) Flow chart B for works by or about more than one author.

(3) Flow chart B is given for notation 8 miscellaneous writings.

(1) **Collections of Debates**
808.85 – Collections of speeches (schedule p. 768, V. 3)
808.851-.856 – Specific kinds of speeches
Instruction: Add to base number 808.85 the numbers following – 50 in notation 501-506 from Table T3B, e.g. Debates = 808.85 + ~~50~~3 (T3B)
Class Number = 808.853

(2) **Literature from specific periods: 809.01 - .05**
Add to base number 809.0 the numbers following –090 in notation 0901-0905 from Table 1, e.g. history, description, critical appraisal of 18th century literature 809.033
809.0 + ~~090~~33 (T1 – 18th century)
809.033

*When language is not given then period has to be taken from Table 1 (SS)*

**Literature for and by persons of general and large western ethnic and national groups**

(3) **Literature by North Americans**
809.8 = Literature for and by specific kinds of persons
809.805-.879: Literature for and by persons of general and larger western ethnic and national groups
Instruction: Add to base number 809.8 notation 05-79 from Table 5
North American = 1 (T5)
809.8 + 1
809.81

(4) **Literature for and by persons of other ethnic and national groups (from schedule)**
Jewish Literature
–809.889 = Persons of other ethnic and national groups
Instruction:
Add to base number 809.889 the numbers following –9 in notation 91-99 from Table 5
–924 = Jews (T5)
809.889 + ~~9~~24
Class number = 809.889 24

(5) **Literature displaying specific features**
809.9 = Literature displaying specific features
809.91 -92 – Literature displaying specific qualities and elements
Add to base number 809.9 notation 1-2 from Table T3C, e.g. History, description, critical appraisal of literature displaying tragedy and horror.
–16 = Tragedy and horror (T3C)
809.9 + 16 (T3C)
Class number = 809.916

(6) **809.933 = Literature dealing with specific themes and subjects**
Instruction:
Add to base number 809.933 the numbers following –3 in notation 32-38 from Table T3C, e.g. History, critical appraisal, description of literature dealing with marriage.
–3543 = Marriage (3TC)
809.933 + ~~3~~543 (marriage)
809.933 543

(7) **Literature Emphasizing Subjects**

Works not basically discussed as literature, in which real interest is in the literary quality of the text rather than the subject of the text.

809.935 = Literature Emphasizing Subjects

Instruction: Add to base number 809.935 notation 001-999, e.g.

Religion = 200

Religious Works as Literature 809.935 + 200 (redundant Zeroes)

Class number = 809.935 2

Biography and autobiography as literature = 809.935 + 920

Class number = 809.935 92 (p. 772)

Depiction of Buddhism in British fiction of 20th century

82 = Base number for British Literature

–3 = Fiction

91 = 20th century

82 + 3 + 91

823.91

**Critical Appraisal of Literary Forms and Specific Periods.**

(1) **Critical Appraisal of Epic Poetry of Elizabethan Period.**

82 – Base number for English

1 – Poetry (T3B)

–1032 – Epic Poetry (T3B)

–11-19 – Poetry of specific periods.

Add to –1 notation from the period table of English 820, e.g. Elizabethan period = 3; then add 0 (Zero) and to the result add further as instructed under –1 –8

–1 –8

–9 – Critical Appraisal

3 = Elizabethan Period

So class number is 82 + 1032 (T3B) + 3 + 0 + 9

821.032 309

(2) **Similarly Critical Appraisal of Punjabi Comedy in Modern Period**

891.42 – Punjabi Literature

–20523 – *Comedy (T3B)

–21-29 – Drama of specific periods
Add to –2 from the period table for specific literature in 810-890, e.g.
Modern period under 891.4 is 72. Then add 0 and to the result add further as instructed under –1–8
09 = critical appraisal (Under 1-8)
72 – Modern period (2000) under 891.49 (p. 807, V. 3)
891.42 + 20523 +72 + 0 + 09
891.422 052 372 09

(3) **Critical Appraisal of Hindi Short Stories on Love of 21st Century**
Base number Hindi Literature = 891.43
Short Stories = 301
21st century = 72 (time period from schedule)
Instruction under –31-39 fiction of specific periods
Add to –3 notation from the period table for specific literature in 810-890
And then add 0 and to the result add further as instructed under –1-8
0 = (CS, T3B, V. 1, p. 633)
9 = Critical Appraisal (p. 627, V. 1, T3B)
Under 91-99
Add to 9 notation 1-9 from Table 3C (V. 1, p. 627, T3B)
3543 = Love and Marriage (T3C)
So Class number = 891.43 + 301 + 72 + 0 + 9 + 3543
891.433 017 209 354 3

(4) **Critical Appraisal Hindi Essays on Romanticism of 20th Century**
891.43 = Hindi Literature
4 = Essays (T3B)
41-49 = Essays of specific periods
Add to-4 notation from the period table for specific literature in 810-890 and then add 0, and to the result add further as instructed under-1-8
9 = Critical Appraisal
Under 91-99
Add to 9 notation 1-9 from Table 3C (V. 1, p. 627, T3B)
71 = 20th century from schedule

145 = (Romanticism T3C)
891.43 + 4 + 71 + 0 + 9 + 145
891.434 710 914 5
(p. 634, T3B)

(5) **Critical Appraisal of Women in Greek Speeches of Ancient Period (earliest period)**
–51–59 = speeches of specific period (p. 635, V. 1)
88 + 5 + 1 + 0 (p. 635, V. 1) + 9 + 92837 (T3C, Women)
885.109 928 37

(6) **Critical Appraisal of Greek Letters of Medieval Periods on Specific Persons**
88 – Base number for Greek Letters
6 – Letters
2 – Period table under 880.1 – 888 (p. 803, V. 3)
0 – CS (T3B) under 61-69 letters of specific periods (p. 635, V. 1)
9 – Critical appraisal (from 91-99 under -1-8 of T3B on p. 627, V. 1)
351 – Specific persons T3C
So = 88 + 6 + 2 + 0 + 9 + 351
886.209 351

(7) **Critical Study of Punjabi Satirical Poetry of 20th Century on Birth**
891.42 = Punjabi Literature
107 = *Satirical Poetry
(Because there is asterisk add as instructed under -102-107)
09 = Critical appraisal
71 = 20th Century
354 = Birth (T3C)
891.42 + 107 (T3B) + 71 + 09 + 354 (T3C) (Birth)
891.421 077 109 354

In all above-mentioned examples literary forms and its subdivisions are of specific period. So formula for these examples is
Base number + form + period + notation 08 or 09 + T3C
If collections or critical appraisal of texts displaying specific features or emphasizing specific subjects for and

by specific kinds of persons then add to 08 or 09 notation 1-9 from Table 3C. Table T3B is further extendable by Table T3C.

(9) **Criticism of Hindi Poetry of 20th Century by Punjabis**
891.43 = Hindi Literature
1 = Poetry
71 = (1940-1999)
09 = Critical Appraisal (as under -1-8, T3B)
8 = (Under -8 add to -8 notation 05-99 from Table 5) (Ethnic group T3C)
9142 = (Punjabi, T5)
891.43 + 1 + 71 + 09 + 8 + 9142
891.431 710 989 142

(9) **Collection of Bengali Literature for Children**
891.44 + 80 (T3B under -1-8 from 801-809) + 9282 (Children) (T3C)
891.448 092 82

(10) **A Critical Appraisal of the Aristotle's Poetics (early period)**
82 = Base Number for English
1 = Poetry (T3B)
1 = Time period from schedule Early English Periods (Aristotle)
09 = According to instruction given under
(-11-19) = Poetry of specific periods
Add to -1 notation from the period table for the specific literature in 810-890. Earliest period -11; then add 0 and to the result add as instructed under -1-8
9 = Critical Appraisal
82 + 1 + 1 (Specific Period) +0 (T3B) +9 (T3B)
821.109
Similarly

(11) **Criticism Spenser's fairy queen**
82 + 1 + 3 + 0 + 9
821.309

(12) **Criticism of words worth's poetry (Elizabethan period)**
82 + 1 + 3 + 09
821.309

### Table 3

**When no language is given time period is taken from Table 1.**

**(1) Criticism of Epic Poetry of Twentieth Century**

808.81 – Collection of poetry

808.812-817 – specific kinds of poetry

Instruction – Add to base number 808.81 the numbers following -10 in notations 102-107 from Table 3B.

1032 – *3Epic Poetry (T3B)

808.81 + (~~10~~32) T3B

808.8132 + 09

According to instruction under -102-107 specific kind of poetry

09 (T3B) History, description, critical appraisal

Add to 09 notations 001-99 from Table 3C

*In Table 3C (-00901-00905)—Historical Periods (it means use two zeros for SS) (p. 641, V. 1) (When Language is not given use time period from SS.*

0904 = Twentieth Century (SS from Table 1)

00904 instead of 0904

So 808.8132 + 09 + 00904

808.813 209 009 04

Similarly

**(2) Collection of Narrative Poetry of Twentieth Century**

808.81 + ~~10~~3 (T3B) + 09 (T3B) + 00904 (T3C)

808.813 090 090 4

Use of T3 = Base number + form + time period from schedule

**(3) English Poetry by Author of Twentieth Century**

Base number for English = 82

Poetry = 1 (T3A)

Twentieth century = 91 (schedule) under 820.1-828

So, Class number = 82 + 1 + 91 = 821.91

821.91

### Use of Table 3 (V. 1, pp. 23-25)

Following examples are given for basic number building for works in an individual language about individual authors (with use of Table 3A and by or about more than one author (with use of Table T3). T3 refers to both Table 3A (individual authors) and Table 3B (more than one author).

**(1) Base number + notation 08 or 09**

**An Anthology of American Literature**

Base Number = 81 for American Literature

08 (T3B) = collections of literary texts in more than one form.

Class Number = 81 + 08 = 810.8

*This is an example of works by or about more than one author, not restricted by period or form (Table 3B).*

**(2) Works by or about more than one author, restricted to a specific period but not to a specific form (Table 3B).**

Formula for this = Base number + notation 08 or 09 + period,
e.g. A collection of 18th century German literature
83 – Base number for German Literature
08 – T3B – Collections of literary texts in more than one form
6 – 18th century from schedule (from period table for German literature, p. 783, V. 3).

Under Table 3B, there is an instruction; use period notation 08001-08009 and 09001-09009 only if there is an applicable period table. So under German language there is an applicable period table use 006 instead of 6.

Class number = 83 + 08 + 006
830.800 6
Similarly

**(A) A collection of French literature of 19th century (7 = 19th century from schedule)**

84 + 08 + 007
840.800 7
Similarly

**(B) Collection of Swedish Literature of 19th Century**

839.7 = Base Number for Swedish Literature
08 = Collection (T3B)

Instruction under Table 3B = Use period notation 08001-08009 and –09001-09009 only if there is an applicable period table.

In applicable period table for Swedish Literature, number is 3 = 17th Century

According to Instruction = 003 instead of 3

So Class Number = 839.7 + 08 + 003

839.708 003

**(3) Works by or about more than one author not restricted by form or period, place of authorship emphasized (T3B)**

Formula for this = Base number + notation 08 or 09 + 9 (T3C) + area notation from Table 2.

An Anthology of Literature of Portuguese by Brazilian Authors

869.080 981

869 – Base for Portuguese Literature

08 – From (T3B)

Instruction under -08- collection of literary texts in more than one form.

080001 – 08099 Add to -080 notation 001-99 from Table 3C (p. 625, V. 1, T3B).

–9 literatures for and by other specific kind of persons (p. 649, V. 1, T3C).

–81 (T2) – Brazil

So Class Number = 869 + 080 + 9 + 81

869.080 981

Similarly

**An Anthology of Frisian Literature by Canadian authors = 839.2080971**

839.2 – Base number for Frisian literature

08 (T3B) – Collection of literary texts of more than one form instruction under 080001-08099 in (T3B)

Add to – 080 notation 001-99 from Table T3C.

–9 (T3C) = Literature for and by other specific kind of persons

–71 = Canada T2 (Area Table)

839.2 + 080 + 9 + 71

839.208 097 1

**Forms T3-1-7 (Table 1, V. 1) p. 24**

**(1) Works by or about an individual author: Restricted to a specific form and period (Table 3A)**

Formula = Base number + form + period

Spenser's Fairy Queen

82 = Base number
–1 = Poetry
3 = (Elizabethan Period, V. 3)
82 + 1 + 3
821.3
Keats Poetry = 82 + 1 + 7 (time period from V. 3)
821.7

**(2) Works by or about more than one author: Restricted to a specific form but not to a specific period (T3B)**

Base number + form + notation 008 or 009
Criticism of English Drama
82 + 2 + 009 = 822.009
Explanation:
82 = Base Number for English
–2 = Drama
–2001-2009 (p. 630, V. 1)
Add to -200 as instructed under -1-8
Under -1-8
9 = Critical appraisal
82 + 200 + 9
822.009

**(3) Works by or about more than one author: Restricted to a specific form, to a specific kind, scope, or medium and to a specific period (T3B)**

Formula for this kind of title is as follows:

Base number + form + kind, scope, or medium + notation 08 or 09 + period

**A collection of 19th Century French short stories**
84 = French Literature
–3 = Fiction
301 = *Short Stories
As it is asterisk follow instructions under -102-107
Under –02-107
08 = Collections of Literary texts
07 = 19th Century (p. 790, V. 3)
84 + 3 + 01 + 08 + 07 = 843.010807
843.010 807
Similarly

(a) **A collection of German Short Stories of 19th Century**
83 + 3 + 01 + 08 + 07
833.010 807

(4) **Works by or about more than one author: Restricted to specific form but not to a specific kind, scope, or medium, restricted to a specific period (T3B)**

Base number + form + period + notation 08 or 09
Criticism of German Drama of the second half of 20th Century
83 + 2 + 914 + 09 = 832.91409
Explanation of above title
83 = (Base number German)
2 = Drama (form)
914 = (2nd half of 20th century from period table of Schedule)
09 = (Criticism)
83 + 2 + 914 + 09
832.914 09

**Form T3-8 miscellaneous writings**

(1) **Works if there are works by or an individual author which is restricted to a specific form and period and also subform is there (T3A-8)**

Formula is = Base number + form + period + subform
**A Collection of Quotations of an individual American author of the later 19th Century**
81 = American Literature
–8 = Miscellaneous Writings (T3B)
4 = (1867-1899), (p. 774, V. 3) from period table.
02 = (quotations, T3B)
81 + 8 + 4 + 02
818.402

**Explanation of above title**

= 81 (Base number American literature) +8 (Miscellaneous Form) +4 (Period Table) +02 (quotations, T3B)

Similarly, a collection of English jokes by an individual English author of Victorian period

82 (Base number for English literature) +8 (Miscellaneous writings and T3B) +8 (Victorian Period) +02 (Jokes, T3B)

828.802

**(2) Works by or about more than one author: Restricted to specific form, period, and subform (T3B-8)**

Base number + form + period + subform + notation 08 or 09

**A Collection of quotations of several French authors of the late 20th Century**

French 84 (Base number for French) +8 (Misc. Writing) +914 (late 20th century) +02 (Quotations, T3B) +08 (Collection)

84 = Base number for French

–8 = Miscellaneous Writings

914 = from time period from schedule

02 = Quotations (T3B)

0201 – 0209 = Standard Subdivisions, Collections....

Add to 020 as instructed under -1-8, e.g. Collections 0208

–08 = Collections (SS)

84 + 8 + 914 + 02 + 08

848.914 020 8

Similarly 83 + 8 + 914 + 02 + 08 (A collection of epigrams of German authors of 19th century)

838.914 020 8

**(3) A collection of English short stories dealing with places**

82 – Base number for English Literature

301 – *Short Stories (T3B)

Instruction under 301-308

Add each subdivision identified by * (asterisked) as instructed under 102-107

Under 102-107

Instruction add to 08 notation 001 to 99 from T3C

32 – Places (T3C)

So 82 (Base number schedule) +301 (Short Stories) +08 (Collections) +32 (Places)

So Class number = 823.010 832

**(4) A collection of Punjabi Literature with love and marriage theme**

891.42 – Base number for Punjabi Literature

08 – T3B-Collections of Literary texts in more than one form

Under 080001-08009 – Add to 080 notation 001-99 from Table 3C (p. 625, V. 1)

3543 – Love & Marriage (T3C)

891.42 (Base number Punjabi) +080 (Collection, T3B) +3543 (Love and Marriage)

So Class Number = 891.420 803 543

**(5) Collections of English Fiction dealing with places**

82 – Base number for English Literature

3 – Fiction – T3B

Instruction under 3001-3009

Add to 300 as instructed under 1-8

Instruction under -1-8

801-809- Collections displaying specific features or emphasizing specific subjects for and by specific kinds of persons. (p. 627, V. 1)

Instruction: Add to 80 notations 1-9 from Table 3C, e.g. collections dealing with places 8032

80 (T3B) + 32 (T3C)

82 (Base number for English literature) +300 (T3B) +80 (T3B) +32 (Places, T3C)

So Class Number = 823.008 032

**(6) Collections of poetry (forms of poetry identified by *collections of poetry of each subdivision identified by *) like dramatic poetry, narrative poetry, epic poetry, sonnets, odes, ballads, etc. all are identified with *. We follow the instructions given under-102-107. We will use 08 and T3C like collections dealing with places 0832, e.g.**

Collections of English Sonnets dealing with places

82 (Base number Schedule) +1042 (Sonnets T3B) +08 (Collections T3B) +32 (Places T3C)

821.042 083 2

Similarly collections of Drama of specific media, scopes, kinds under 202-205

Add to each sub division identified by *(from 202-205) as instructed under 102-107 – e.g. collections of comedies dealing with places = 205230832

**(7) Collections of English tragedy of places**

82 (Base number from schedule) +20512 (Tragedy, T3B) +08 (Collection, T3B) +32 (Places, T3C)

822.051 208 32

Similarly collections of fiction (301-308) of scopes and kinds (p. 632, V. 1)

Add to each sub division identified by * as instructed under 102-107, e.g.

**(8) Collections of American Horror fiction of all times.**

81 (Base number American Literature) +308738 (T3B Horror Fiction) +08 (Collection T3B) +33 (Times T3C)

813.087 380 833

Formula for all above-mentioned titles is as follow

Base number + form + subform + 08 + T3C

### For Speeches

**(9) Collections of French Debates dealing with places**

84 (Base number of French Literature) +503 (Debates T3B) +08 (Collections 08 T3B) +32 (Places T3C)

845.030 832

**(10) Collections of French Recitations dealing with all times**

84 + 504 + 08 + 33

845.040 833

**(11) Collections of Greek Public Speeches (Oratory) dealing with places**

88 (Base number Greek literature) +501 (Public Speeches T3B) +08 (collection T3B) +32 (Places T3C)

About titles for * forms of poetry, drama, fiction and speeches, etc.

Now for all the standard forms of literature like poetry, drama, fictions, essays, speeches, letters, human and satire, when we use standard subdivisions, we add to

100 in case of poetry

200 in case of drama

300 in case of fiction

400 in case of essays

500 in case of speeches

600 in case of letters

700 in case of humor and satire as instructed under 1-8, e.g.

Collections of humor and satire dealing with places = 700 + 80 + 32 = 700 803 2 (p. 636, V. 1)

Explanation of above number

–7 = Humor and satire

–700 1- 700 9= standard subdivisions; collections; History; description; critical appraisal

Add to -700 as instructed under -1-8, e.g.

Under -1-8

801-809 = collections displaying specific features or emphasizing specific subjects, for and by specific kinds of persons

Add to 80 notation 1-9 from Table 3C, e.g. collections dealing with places = 8032

–32 = places (T3C)

700 + 80 + 32 = 700 803 2

**(12) Collections of essays dealing with places**

= 400 + 80 + 32 = 4008032

Speeches dealing with times = 500 + 80 + 33 = 5008033

Fiction dealing with all times = 300 + 80 + 33 = 3008033

Drama – Places = 200 + 80 + 32 = 2008032

**Literature for and by specific kinds of persons**

**(13) Collections of Punjabi Novels by rural authors**

891.42 – Base number for Punjabi Literature

–3 – Novels (T3B)

Instruction – Add to –300 as instructed under 1-8

Collection displaying specific features – 801-809 (T3B)

Instruction: – Add to 80 notation 1-9 from Table 3C

–91 – Literature for and by persons resident in specific regions (p. 649, V. 1)

Instruction: – Add to –91 the numbers following –1 in notations 11-19 from Table 2

–1734 – Rural (Table 2)

891.42 + 300 + 80 + 91 + 1734

891.423 008 091 734

**(13) Collections of Hindi Written by Gay-Men**

891.42 – Base number Hindi Literature

–92- Literature for and by persons of specific classes

Add to –920 the number following –08 in notation 085-087 from Table 1

08664 – Gay-Men

891.42 + 920 + ~~08~~664

891.429 206 64

Literature for and by persons of specific classes

**(15) Collections of Bengali Poetry by persons in late adulthood**

891.44 – Base number for Bengali Poetry

–1 = Poetry (T3B)

Inst. Add to 100 as instructed -1-8

801 – 809 = Collections displaying specific features or emphasizing specific subjects, for and by specific kinds of persons (T3B)

Inst. Add to 80 notation 1-9 from T3C.

9285 = persons in late adulthood (T3C)

92 – Literature for and by persons and specific classes (T3C)

928 – Persons of specific age groups and sexes (T3C)

9285 – Persons in late adulthood (T3C)

891.44 + 100 + 80 + 9285

891.441 008 092 85

**(16) Collection of English Poetry Literature by men**

82 + 100 + 80 + 9286 (T3C)

821.008 092 86

Literature for and by persons resident in specific continents, countries, localities

**(17) Collection of Urdu Poetry by the residents of Australia**

891.439 – Base number for Urdu Literature

–1 – Poetry (T3B)

Inst. Add to 100 as instructed under -1-8

–1–8 Inst = Add to 80 notation 1-9 from Table 3C.

–93-99 Literature for and by persons resident in specific countries, continents, localities

Add to 9 notation 3-9 from Table 2

–94 – Australia (T2)

So 891.439 (Base number Urdu Literature) +100 (Poetry T3B) +80 (T3B) +9 (T3C) +94 (T2)

891.439 100 809 94

**(18) Collection of English Literature by Residents of Japan**

82 + 080 + 9 + 52

82 – Base number English Literature

08 – Collection of Literary texts in more than one form

08001-08099 – Inst. Add to 080 notation 001-99 from (T3C)

93-99 – Literature for and by persons resident in specific continents, countries, localities

Inst. Add to –9 notation 3-9 from Table 2.

–52 – For Japan in (T2)

82 + 080 + 9 + 52

820.809 52

Similarly

**(19) Literature by residents of Hokkaido in Japanese Language**

895.6 – Base number – Japanese Literature

08 – Collections of Literary texts in more than one form.

Inst: Add to 080 notation 001-99 from T3C.

–93-99 Literature for and by persons in specific country, continent and locality

Inst: Add to –9 notation 3-9 from Table 2.

524 – Hokkaido

Class Number = 895.6 (Base number Japanese Literature) +080 (T3B Collections) +9 (T3C) +524 (T2 Hokkaido)

895.608 095 24

**Literature by specific occupational and religions groups**

**(20) Collections of English Literature by Catholics**

82 (Base number for English) +080 (T3B) +921 (T3C) +282 (Roman Catholic from Catholics)

820.809 212 82

Similarly

**(21) Collection of American Literature by painters**

81 (Base number American English) +080 (T3B) +921 (T3C) +750 (Painting)

810.80921750

810.809 217 5

–8 Literature for and by persons of ethnic and national groups

**(22) Collection of Chinese literature written by Punjabis**

895.1 – Chinese Literature

–08 – Collections of Literary texts (T3B)

Instruction – Add to 080 notation 001-99 from Table 3C.

Literature for and by persons of ethnic and national groups (T3C)

Add to –8 notation 05-99 from Table 5

9142 – Punjabi (T5)

So Class number = 895.1 (Base number for Chinese Language) +080 (T3B collection) +8 (T3C person of descent) +9142 (T5 Punjabi)

895.108 089 142

Literature emphasizing philosophic and abstract themes.

**(23) Collection of English Literature on Buddhism**

82 + 080 + 382 + 2943

82 – Base number for English Literature

08 – Collections of literary texts (T3B)

Instruction – Add to 080 notation 001-99 from T3C

–38 – Philosophic and abstract themes T3C

382 – Religious Themes

Instruction = Add to 382 the numbers following 2 in 201-290

Buddhism = 294.3

So Class number = 82 + 080 + 382 + 2943

= 820.803 829 43

**(24) Depiction of Hinduism in British Fiction**

82 + 300 (T3B) +9 (T3B) +382 (T3C) +2945 (Hinduism)

823.009 382 945

Collections of literary texts from more than two literatures.

The collections of literary texts from more than two literatures are to be classified under 808.

**(25) Collections from 20th Century Literature**

808.8 = Collections of Literary texts from more than two literatures.

8001-8005 – Collections from specific periods

Instruction: Add to base number 808.800 the numbers following -090 in notation 0901-0905 from Table 1 (p. 767, V. 3 Schedule)

0904 – 20th century (T1)

Classification number is = 808.800 + 0904

808.800 4

(Period has been taken from general period table from Table 1)

In this title, no language and form is given so here we will use time period from Table 1.

**Collections displaying specific features** = 801-803 (Schedule)

Inst: Add to Base number 808.80 notation 1-3 from T3C.

**(26) Collection of Literature on Death**

808.80 = Collection of Literature

3548 = Death (T3C)

808.80 + 3548

808.803 548

**(27) Collections of Literature Featuring Classicism**

808.80 + 142

808.801 42

**(2) Specific Kind of Poetry, Drama, Fiction and Speeches [p. 167 of V. 1, Table]**

The add instructions of 808.812 – .818 specific kinds of poetry, which allows the addition of the number following (T3B) –10 in notation 102-107 from T3B also permit further addition at that point, since numbers in the range T3B-102-107 have a footnote that leads to an add table under a centered entry. "Add as instructed under T3B-102-107".

Do not add notation 08 collection of literary texts from the add table under T3B-102-107 by itself, since it would be redundant because 808-08 already means collections of literary texts. For example

**(28) Collections of Narrative Poetry**

808.81 – collections of poetry

812-817 specific kinds of poetry

Add to base number 808.81 the numbers following -10 in notation

102-107 from Table 3B

103 – Narrative poetry

Class number = 808.81 + ~~10~~3

808.813

However, add notation 08 if it serves as a link for adding further notation from Table 3C, e.g. collections of narrative Poetry about Political themes = 808.813 083 58 (p. 167, V. 1).

**(29) Collections of Tragedies**

808.82 – collection of drama

822-825 – specific media, scopes, kinds of drama

Inst: Add to base number 808.82 the numbers following –20 in notation 202-205 from Table T3B

20512 – Tragedies (T3B)

Class Number – 808.82 + ~~20~~512

808.825 12

Similarly

**(30) Collections of Love Stories**

808.83 – Collections of Fictions

831-838

Add to base number 808.83 the numbers following 30 in notation

301-308 from Table 3b

3085 – Love Stories (3b)

808.83 + ~~30~~85

808.838 5

**(31) Collections of Descriptive Essays**

808.84 – collections of essays

808.849 – essays displaying specific features

Inst: Add to base number 808.849 notation 1-3 from Table 3C

88- T3C – description

808.849 + 22

808.849 22

**(32) Critical appraisal of Punjabi dramatic poetry by Bengalis**

891.42 – Base number

102 – *Dramatic Poetry

Add as instructed Under 102-107 specific kinds of poetry

09 – Critical appraisal

Add to 09 notation 001-99 from Table T3C

–8 – Literature for and by persons of ethnic and national groups (T3C)

Add to -8 notation from Table 5

9144 – Bengali T5

Class number is 891.42 + 102 + 09 + 8 + 9144

891.421 020 989 144

**(33) Himachal Pradesh as depicted in Hindi Poetry**

891.43 = Base number for Hindi Literature

–1 = Poetry

–1001–1009

Inst: Add to 100 as instructed under -1-8

Collections displaying specific features 801-809

Inst: Add to 80 notation 1-9 from Table 3C

Places (T3C) – 32

Inst: Add to 32 notation 1-9 from Table 2

Himachal Pradesh – 5452

Class Number = 891.43 + 100 + 80 + 32 + 5452

891.431 008 032 545 2

This table can also be used with some base numbers in 700.4, 791.4, 808-809

**(1) Comedian Films**

791.4361-Films displaying specific qualities

Add to base number no. 791.4361 the numbers following –1 in notation 11-17 from T3C

791.4361 + ~~1~~7

791.436 17

**(2) Collections of Letters displaying classicism**

808.869 = Letters displaying specific features

Add to base number 808.869 notation 1-3 from Table 3C

–142 = classicism (T3C)

808.869 + 142

808.869 142

**(3) Historical themes in the Arts**

700.42.48 = Arts dealing with themes and subjects

Add to base number 700.4 the numbers following –3 in notation 32-38 from Table 3C

700.4 + ~~3~~58

700.458

## Reference

1. Dewey Decimal Classification and Relative Index: /devised by Melvil Dewey.- 22nd /edited by John s. Mitchell et al., Dublin, OH: OCLC, V. 1, pp. 616-17.

# 7

# Use of Subdivisions of Individual Languages and Language Families (Table 4)

### Use of Table 4 Languages (Dictionaries)

DDC contains subdivisions for individual languages in Table 4. Notation in Table 4 is never used alone, but may be used as required by add notes under subdivisions of specific languages or languages families, or with the base numbers for individual languages identified by *as explained under 420-490 in Schedule. A point is inserted following the third digit of any number, constructed, that is longer than three digits. This is very simple to use as compare to literature (T3). Notation given in this table is used for main class 400 (Languages) and is supplemented by Table 6.

It is given under 420-490, Table 4 notation can be used with* (asterisk) marked numbers.

Look in schedules to find the base number for the languages. Base number can be identified in an add note, e.g. (for English base number is 42).

Under 420.1-428 add to base number 42 notation 01-8 from Table 4 or another note e.g. At 430.1-438 add to base number 491.43 notation 01-8 from Table 4. This rule has been clarified in DDC footnote and it has been explained by giving a foot note for each zero (0) ending number. In Table 6, subdivision for languages has been given. When an instruction is given only, then we should use notation of Table 6.

Class Dictionaries of Standard form of language in –3 (T4)

**"Do not use SS 03 for dictionaries of languages. Languages have their own Table 4. In Table 4 (–3) is used for dictionaries. Numbers from Table 4 always added to the 'base number' from schedule. Do not add from Table 4, if a language is not recognized as a base number from schedule. For example,**

**Dictionary of old Spanish = 467.01"**

(A)

(1) **Dictionary of Hindi Language**
Base number for Hindi = 491.43
–3 (T4) = Dictionary of standard form of language
Class number = 491.43 + 3 = 491.433

(2) **Etymology of Punjabi**
491.42 = Base number for Punjabi Language
–2 (T4) = Etymology of standard form of language
Class number = 491.42 + 2
491.422

(3) **English Grammar = 425**
42 = Base number for English
–5 (T5) = Grammar of standard form of language
425

(4) **Nouns in English Language**
42 = Base number for English
–554 = nouns (T4)
Class number = 42 + 554
425.54

(5) **Tenses in American English**
41 = Base number for American English
–562 = Tense (T4)
Class number = 41 + 562
415.62
Always remember, insert a point (decimal point) after first three digits in a constructed class number.

(6) **Word formation in French Language**
44 = Base number for French
–592 = word formation (T4)
Class number = 44 + 592
Class number = 445.92

(7) **Dictionary of Synonymies and Antonyms of Spanish**
46 = Base number for Spanish
–312 (T4) = dictionary of synonymies and antonyms
Class number = 46 + 312
463.12

(8) **Dictionary of Punjabi Idioms**
491.42 = base number for
Punjabi
–313 (T4) = Idioms
Class number = 491.42 + 313
491.423 13

(9) **Picture Dictionaries in Romanian**
459 = base number for Romanian
–317 (T4) = picture dictionary
Class Number = 459 + 317
459.317

(10) **Adverbs in English Dictionaries**
42- Base number for English
–576 (T4) = Adverbs
Class number = 42 + 576
425.76
Formula for above-mentioned titles is
Base Number + Table 4

**(B) Almost all the languages have words of other languages in it. Titles like Greek words in English, Sanskrit words in Punjabi, etc. In this title a language contains foreign element in it.**

(1) **Sanskrit words in Punjabi**
Base number for Punjabi = 491.42
Foreign Element = –24 (T4)
Instruction: Add to –24 Notations 1-9 from Table 6.
–912 (T4) = Sanskrit
Class number = 491.42 + 24 + 912
491.422 491 2

(2) **French words in English Language**
42 = French Language
Foreign Element = –24 (T4)
Add to –24 notation 1-9 from Table 6.

French Language = 41 (T6)
Class number = 42 + 24 + 41
422.441

(3) **Translation from Russian Language to Punjabi Language**
Base Number for Punjabi = 491.42
–802 = Translating to and from other languages
Inst.: Add to –802 notation 2-9 from Table 6 for the language being translated from
9171 (T6) = Russian Language
Class Number = 491.42 + 802 + 9171
491.428 029 171

(4) **Translation from Urdu to Punjabi**
491.42 = Punjabi
–802 = Translating to and from other Language
Inst.: Add to –802 notation 2-9 from Table 6 for language being translated from
91439 = Urdu (T6)
Class number = 491.42 + 802 + 91439
491.428 029 143 9

(5) **Structural approach to expression of English for Punjabi speaking people**
42 = Base number for English Language
–824 (T4) = Structural approach to expression for persons whose native language is different.
Inst.: Add to -824 notation 2-9 from Table 6.
–9142 (T6) = Punjabi Language
Class Number = 42 + 824 + 9142
428.249 142

(6) **Structural approach to expression of Spanish for Russian speaking people**
46 = Base number for Spanish Language in schedule (p. 909)
–824 (T4) = Structural approach to expression for persons whose native language is different.
–9171 (T6) = Russian Language
Class Number = 46 + 824 + 9171
468.249 171

(7) **Audio Lingual Approach to expression of French for Hindi Speaking People**
44 = Base number for French
–834 = Audio Lingual approach to expression for persons whose native language is different.
Inst.: Add to –834 notation 2-9 from Table 6
–9143 = Hindi (T6)
Class Number = 44 + 834 + 9143
448.349 143

(8) **Words in English**
42 = Base number for English
–81 = Words (T4)
Class Number = 42 + 81
428.1

(9) **Spellings and Pronunciation of Urdu Language**
491.439 = Base number for Urdu
–813 = Spellings and Pronunciation
Class Number = 491.439 + 813 (T4)
491.439 813

(10) **Spanish Primers (readers)**
46 = Base number for Spanish
–86 = Readers (T4)
Class Number = 46 + 86
468.6

(11) **English Reader Book**
42 = Base number for English
–86 = Readers (T4)
Class number = 42 + 86 = 428.6

(12) **British Systems of singing and finger spelling of English**

42 = Base number

89 = Use of spoken language or a manually coded form of a spoken language of communication with and by deaf persons.

891.4-891.9: specific systems of manual coding.

Inst.: Add to base number –891 notation 4-9 from Table 2 for supranational region or county only.

–41 = Britain (T2)

So Class number = 42 + 891 + 41

428.914 1

(13) **Lip reading of Spanish Language.**

46 = Base number of Spanish

–8954 (T4) = Lip Reading

Class Number = 46 + 8954

468.954

# 8

# Use of Ethnic and National Groups (Table 5)

The following numbers are never used alone, but may be used as required (either directly when so noted or through the interposition of notation 089 from Table 1) with any number from the schedules, e.g. civil and political rights (323.11) of Navajo Indians (–9726 in this table): 323.119726; ceramic arts (738) of Jews (–924 in this table): 738.089924. They may also be used when so noted with numbers from other tables, e.g. notation 174 from Table 2.

In this table, racial groups are mentioned in connection with a few broad ethnic groupings, e.g. a note to class Blacks of African origin at –96 Africans and people of African descent. Concepts of race vary. A work that emphasizes race should be classed with the ethnic group that most closely matches the concept of race described in the work.

Except where instructed otherwise, and unless it is redundant, add 0 to the number from this table and to the result and notation 1 or 3-9 from Table 2 for area in which a group is or was located, e.g. Germans in Brazil –31081, but Germans in Germany –31; Jews in Germany or Jews from Germany –924043. If notation from Table 2 is not added, use 00 for standard subdivisions; see below for complete instructions on using standard subdivisions.

Notation from Table 2 may be added if the number in Table 5 is limited to speakers of only one language even if the group discussed does not approximate the whole of the group specified by the Table 5 number, e.g. Bavarians in Brazil -31081 (because German is the primary language spoken by Bavarians), but

Amhara in United States –928 (not –928073 because Amharic is not the only language spoken by the peoples included in –928)

Notation from Table 2 may be added for either present or past specific location of the group discussed if only one specific location of the group discussed if only one specific location is relevant, e.g. sociology of Jews from many different countries now in United States 305.8924073, contributions to music around the world of Jews who previously lived in Poland 780.899240438.

If both present and past specific locations of the group discussed are relevant, then notation from Table 2 is added only for present location of the group, e.g. Jews from Germany in the United States –924073 (not –924043). An exception occurs when the present location of the group is defined by the class number to which ethnic or national group notation is added, e.g. Jews in United States history 973.04924. The area notation added to Table 5 numbers is then available to show the past location of the group, e.g. Jews from German in United States history 973.04924043, Jews from Germany in United States higher education 378.73089924043.

Standard subdivisions may be added to Table 5 notation when that notation is added directly to the base number, e.g. periodicals about sociology of Irish Americans 305.8916207305. However, standard subdivisions are not added to Table 5 notation when that notation is used through interposition of notation 089 from Table 1, e.g. an exhibition of ceramic arts of Russian Jews 738.089924047 (not 738.089924047074).

**Table 5. Ethnic and National Groups (continued)**

When Table 5 notation is not followed by 0 plus notation from Table 2, use 00 for standard subdivisions, e.g. periodicals about sociology of Japanese 305.8956005, collected biography of Irish Americans in New York City 974.71004916200922. When Table 5 notation is followed by 0 plus notation from Table 2, however, use 0 for standard subdivisions, e.g. periodicals about sociology of Japanese Americans 305.895607305. (For the purpose of this rule, notation 96073 African Americans is treated as Table 5 notation, e.g. periodicals on sociology of

African Americans 305.896073005, periodicals on sociology of African Americans in Ohio 305.896073077105.)

Except where instructed otherwise, give preference to ethnic group over nationality, e.g. United States citizens of Serbian descent –91822073 (not -13). In this table "ethnic group" most often means a group with linguistic ties, but it can also mean a group with other cultural ties.

Except where instructed otherwise, when choosing between two ethnic groups, give preference to the group for which the notation is different from that for the nationality of the people, e.g. a work treating equally Hispanic and Native American heritage of bilingual Spanish-Guarani mestizos of Paraguay –983820892 (not –68892).

Except where instructed otherwise, when choosing between two national groups, give preference to the former or ancestral national group, e.g. people from the former Soviet Union who became United States Citizens –917073 (not –13).[1]

**Table 5 is used by following two methods**

1. When instructions are given to add from Table 5 to a base number for ethnic and social group.
2. T5 is also used through standard subdivision 089 when specific instruction is not given but title has the presence of national, social and ethnic group.

(1) **Social Status of Pakistanis**

305.8 = Social structure of Racial Ethnic Group (schedule)
Instruction under 305.805-89 = Specific ethnic and national groups
Add to base number 305.8 notation 05-9 from T5
–914122 = Pakistanis (T5)
305.8 + 914122
305.891 412 2

(2) **Civil Rights of Jews**

323.1 = Civil rights of non-dominant groups
323.11 = Ethnic and national groups

Instruction under 323.111-.119 = specific ethnic and national group
Add to base number 323.11 notation 1-9 from Table 5
Jews = –924
323.11 + 924
323.119 24

(3) **Ethnology of Celts**
599.97 = Human Ethnic Groups (ethnology)
599.98 = Specific ethnic groups
Add to base number 599.98 notation 05-9 from Table 5, e.g. Celts
Celts = 916 (T5)
599.98 + 916
599.989 16

(4) **Civil rights of African Americans**
323.111 = Ethnic and national groups
Instruction under 323.111-.119 = Specific ethnic and national group
Add to base number 323.11 notation 1-9 from Table 5
Africans = 96
Connecting digit = 0
Americans = 73
323.11 + 96 + 0 + 73
323.119 607 3

(5)(1) **Education of Punjabis in Ottawa**
Education of Specific kinds of students = 371.82
Instruction under 371.821-829
(Add to base number 371.82 the numbers following 08- in notation 081-089 from Table 1. Education of students of specific Ethnic or National origin 371.829)
Other Ethnic and National Groups = –9 (p. 667, V. 1 of Table 5)
–089 = Ethnic and National Group (T1)
08905-0899:
Add to base number-089 notation 05-9 from T5 (p. 209, V. 1)

–9142 = Punjabis (T5)
Is further divisible by T5
–71384 = Ottawa
371.82 + ~~089~~ + 9142 + 0 + 71384
371.829 914 207 138 4
Period subdivisions of world history as given under 909.1-909.8 can also be added with zero as facet indicator.

(6) **World History of Jews in the 18th Century**
909.04 = History with respect to ethnic and national group
Instruction:
Add to base number 909.04 notation 05-9 from Table 5, e.g. then add 0 and to the result add the numbers following 909 in 909.1-909.8
Jews = 924 (T5)
909.04 + 924 + 0 + ~~909~~.7
909.049 240 7 (p. 823, V. 3)
Similarly

(7) **World History of Punjabis in 19th century** [9142 (T5) **Punjabis**]
909.04 + 9142 (T5) + 0 + ~~909~~.8
909.049 142 08

(8) **World History of Bhutanese in 1900-1919**
909.04+91418 (T5) + ~~909~~.821
909.049 141 882 1

(9) **Indian Migrant Labor in England**
331 = Labor Economics
331.630 5 – 639 = Specific Native born indigenous ethnic groups
Instruction under 331.630 5-639
Add to base number 331.63 notation 05-9 from Table 5, [e.g. African Americans 331.6396073, African American workers in Alabama 331.63960730761" (p. 427, Schedule)]
Similarly
Indians = –91411 (T5)

0 = Connecting digit
–42 = England
331.63 + 91411 + 0 + 42
331.639 141 104 2

(10) **Indians in USA**
305.8 = Social structure of Racial Ethnic Group (schedule)
Instruction under 305.805-89
Specific ethnic and national groups
Add to base number 305.8 notation 05-9 from T5
–91411 = Indians (T5)
0 = Connecting Digit (From Example p. 337, V. 2)
–73 = USA
305.8 + 91411 + 0 + 73
305.891 411 073

(11) **Ethnic Cookery of Iraqis (Imp. Title)**
Ethnic Cookery = 641.592
Add to base number 641.592 notation 05-9 from Table 5
–9275–9276 = regional and national groups of Arabs (p. 672, V. 1)
Instruction: Add to –927 notation 5-6 from Table 2
567 = Iraq (T2)
Number for Iraqis = 927 + 567 (T2) = 927 567 (no ready made number for Iraqis)
641.592 + 927567
641.592 927 567
Similarly Cookery of Lebananies
641.592 + {927 + 5692 (T2)}
641.592 927 569 2

(12) **Decorative Arts of Indians**
704.03 = History and description with respect to ethnic and national groups
Add to base number 704.03 notation 05-9 from Table 5, e.g. art of North American native peoples 704.0397 (p. 540, V. 3)
–91411 = Indians
704.03 + 91411
704.039 141 1

(13) **Bengalis living in Delhi**
305 = Social Structure
305.8 = Ethnic and National Groups
305.805-89 specific ethnic and national groups
Add to base number 305.8 notation 05-9 from Table 5
e.g.
–9144 = Bengalis (T5)
0 = connecting symbol (e.g. on p. 337, V. 2) (Chinese Australians = 305.8951094)
–5456 = Delhi
305.8 + 9144 + 0 + 5456
305.891 440 545 6

(14) **Ethno Psychology of African Americans**
155.8 = cross culture Psychology
155.84 = specific ethnic groups
Add to the base number 155.84 notation 05-9 from Table 5,
–96 = Africans
0 = connecting digit
–73 = Americans
155.84 + 96 + 0 + 73
155.849 607 3

(15) **Italian National Psychology**
155.89 = National Psychology
Add to base number 155.89 notation 3-9 Table 2,
Italian = 51 (T5)
155.89 + 51
155.895 1

(16) Encyclopedia of Ethnic Cookery of Sikkimese
Ethnic Cookery = 641.592
Add to base number 641.592 notation 05-9 from Table 5
Sikkimese = 91417
–03 = Encyclopedia
641.592 + 91417 + 03
641.592 914 170 3

(17) **Encyclopedia of Spanish Folk Music**

Music of Ethnic group = 789.2

Add to base number 789.2 notation 1-9 from Table 5 e.g. Spanish folk music 789.261 (p. 708, V. 3)

–61 = Spanish (T2)

–0 = Connecting Digit

–03 = Encyclopedia (T1)

789.2 + 61 + 0 + θ3

789.261 03

(18) **Journal of Ethno Psychology of Italians in Japan**

155.84 = Specific Ethnic Groups

Instruction: Add to base number 155.84 notation 05-9 from Table 5

–51 = Italians (T5)

–0 = Connecting digit

–52 = Japan (T2)

155.84 + 51 + 0 + 52

155.845 105 2

(19) **Civil Rights of Punjabis who become US Citizens.**

323.11 = Civil Rights of Ethnic and National groups.

Instruction: Add to base number 323.11 notation 1-9 from Table 5.

Punjabis = 9142

0 = Connecting digit

–73 = USA

323.11 + 9142 + 0 + 73

323.119 142 073

(20) **Collections of Literature by Pakistanis**

808.89 = Collections of Literature by more than one language by persons

Instruction:

Add to base number 808.89 notation 8-9 from T3C Collections of Literature in more than one language by persons. (p. 770), V. 3 of schedule.

–8 = Literature for and by persons of ethnic and national groups (p. 648) of V. 1.

Instruction:
"Add to -8 notation 05-9 from Table 5, e.g. Literature by Africans and persons of African Descent-896" (p. 648, V. 1)
–914122 = Pakistani (T5)
808.89 + 8 + 914122
808.898 914 122

(b) **Use of Table 5 without Instructions**

**When instruction for the use of ethnic and national groups is not given in the schedule, then we can use T5 through SS (–089). There is instruction under –089 in SS Table. See following examples.**

(21) **Migration of Punjabis**
304.8 = Movement of People
No instruction for National Ethnic groups in schedule
–089 = Ethnic and National Groups, [T1 (SS)]
Instruction:
–08905-0899 = Specific ethnic and national groups
Add to base number –089 notation 05-9 from Table 5
–9142 = Punjabis
304.8 + 089 + 9142
304.808 991 42

(22) **Elementary Education of Sri Lankans (Ceylonese)**
372 = Elementary education
No instruction in schedule for National Ethnic groups. So
–089 = Ethnic and National Groups
08905 – 0899 = Specific Ethnic and National Groups
Add to base number-089 notation 05-9 from Table 5
91413 = Sri Lankans (T5)
372 + 089 + 91413
372.089 914 13
Similarly

(23) **Husband-Wife Relations of Estonians**
306.872 = Husband-Wife Relationship
–089 = Ethnic and national groups

08905-0899 = Specific Ethnic and National Groups
Add to base number –089 notation 05-9 from Table 5
Estonians = 945 45
306.872 + 089 + 945 45
306.872 089 945 45

(24) **Higher Education of Indians in USA**
Higher Education = 378
Instruction for using Standard Subdivisions in schedule 378.001-.009 (it means use two zeros instead of one zero while using SS)
–089 = Ethnic and National Groups (T1)
–91411 = Indians (T5)
0 = Connecting digit
–73 = USA
378 + 0089 + 91411 + 0 + 73
378.008 991 411 073

(25) **Child Labor among Indians**
Similarly 331.31 + 089 (T1) + 91411 (T5)
331.310 899 141 1

(26) **Reading habits of Indians in England**
028.9 = Reading interests and habits
–089 = (T1)
–91411 = Indians (T5)
–0 = Connecting symbol
–42 = England
028.9 + 089 + 91411 + 0 + 42
028.908 991 411 042

(27) **Labor Unions of Indians in England**
331.88 = Labor Unions
–089 = (T1)
–91411 = Indians (T5)
0 = Connecting digit
–42 = England
331.88 + 089 + 91411 + 0 + 42
331.880 899 141 104 2

(28) **Directory of Musicians of Ohio**

780.92 = Persons associated with music (musicians)
–025 = Directory (SS)
Instruction: Add to base number 025 notation 1-9 from Table 2 (p. 190, V. 1)
–771 = Ohio (T2)
780.92 + 025 + 771
780.920 257 71

## Reference

1. *Dewey Decimal Classification and Relative Index*, 22nd ed./edited by John S. Mitchell, et al. Dublin: OCLC, 2003, 1-4V, (V. 1) pp. 660-61.

# 9
# Dictionaries and Use of Table 6

## Dictionaries of Languages

There are two types of Dictionaries. One is language dictionaries and other dictionaries are of some specific subjects. We use notation for dictionaries of standard form of language from Table 4. That is –3. But there is also notation for dictionaries in Table 1 (T1) under (–03). In standard subdivision (T1), notation –03 for dictionaries is used for the dictionaries of some specific subjects. We cannot use it for language dictionaries. For language dictionaries can be of three types.

Unilingual dictionaries, bilingual dictionaries and specialized dictionaries. In Unilingual dictionary, the words and its meaning are given in one language, e.g. Hindi dictionary, Punjabi dictionary or English dictionary.

In Bilingual Dictionaries, words are given in one language and its meanings are given in another language, e.g. English – Punjabi Dictionary.

Specialized dictionary means special type of dictionary, e.g. dictionary of idioms, dictionary of synonyms and antonyms, dictionaries of acronyms and abbreviations and picture dictionaries of English. These dictionaries are discussed in chapter named "Use of Table 4".[1]

### Unilingual Dictionaries

(1) **Dictionary of Bengali Language**
491.44
–3 (T4) – Dictionary of standard form of Dictionary

491.44 + 3
491.443

(2) **Dictionary of English**
42 – Base number for English Language
–3 – Dictionary of Standard form of language
Class number = 42 + 3
423

(3) **Dictionary of Punjabi Language**
491.42 – Base number for Punjabi
–3 (T4) – Dictionary of standard form of the language
Class number 491.42 + 3
= 491.423

(4) **Dictionary of Hindi Language**
491.43 – Base number for Hindi
–3 (T4) – Dictionaries of the standard form of the language
Class number = 491.43 + 3
491.433

(5) **Dictionary of Urdu**
= 491.439 + 3 = 491.439 3

(6) **Dictionary of English**
= 42 + 3 = 423

## Use of Table 6

*Bilingual Dictionaries*

For Bilingual dictionaries, there are sufficient rules in DDC for constructing class numbers and base numbers for different languages.

Formula for Bilingual dictionaries is Base number for one language from schedule +3 (T4) + Second Language from T6.

Under –32-39 – Bilingual Dictionaries (p. 655, V. 1)

Instruction: Add to –3 notation 2-9 from Table 6

In Bilingual dictionaries two languages are used. Base number for one language is taken from schedule and other language is taken from Table 6.

(1) **English Telugu Dictionary**
42 – Base number for English from schedule
3 = Dictionary of Standard form of The Language (T-4)
–32-39 Bilingual Dictionaries
Add to –3 notation 2-9 from Table 6
–94827 = Telugu (T6)
Class number will be = 42 + 3 (T4) + 94827 (T6)
423.948 27

(2) **English Hindi Dictionary**
42 = Base number for English
–3 = Dictionary of Standard form of The Language (T4)
–32 – 39 Bilingual Dictionaries
Add to –3 notation 2-9 from Table 6
9143 = T6
Class number = 42 + 3 + 9143
423.914 3

(3) **Dictionary of French and English Language**
44 = Base number for French
–3 = T4
21 – English Language (T6)
So Class number = 44 + 3 + 21
443.21

(4) **Dictionary of Tamil and Hindi**
494.811 – Tamil language
–3 = (T4) – Dictionary of language
9143 (T6) – Hindi
Class number = 494.811 + 3 + 9143
494.811 391 43

(5) **Hindi Tamil Dictionary**
491.43 – Hindi
–3 (T4) – Dictionary
94811 – Tamil
491.433 948 11

(6) **Dictionary of Hindi and Sanskrit**
491.43 – Hindi

–3 = T4 (Dictionary of a Language)
–912 = T6 Sanskrit (Add to -3 notation 2-9 from Table 6)
491.43 + 3 + 912
491.433 912

(7) **Dictionary of Greek and English**
48 = Base number for Greek
–3 = T3b instruction
–21 = English T6
Class number = 48 + 3 + 21
483.21

### Dictionaries of Subjects

–03 (Dictionaries) of Table 1 is used in certain cases for dictionaries of some specific subjects.

*Rules for adding standard subdivisions*

A standard subdivision may be added to any class number. If the ultimate class number is the main class (as in the example philosophy = 100) or a division have two zeroes, then these two filler zeroes are removed while adding the SS from Table 1. In above example dictionary of Philosophy, there are two filler zeroes in Philosophy. So

1~~00~~ + 03 = 103

It should be noted that zero/zeroes removed are those not belonging to the standard sub divisions but the class number. The featured zero of SS is always there. The zero/zeros filling the vacant space are to be removed before adding standard sub divisions and the digits are reshuffled so that the dot (.) is put after first three digits.

The only formula to use standard subdivisions is to follow instructions if any, provided in the schedules under every class number.

In Urdu to avoid confusion, instructions are given in schedules to use one zero, two zero or three zeroes in schedules. See examples.

(1) **Dictionary of Political Science**

320 – Political Science

320.01-09 – Standard Subdivisions

–03 – Dictionary SS (T1)

Class Number = 320 + 03 not 320.3

Here we can't cut filler zero of class number 320 because if we cut 320 + 03, the number will be 320.3 and this number means comparative politics in schedule. So always follow instructions given in schedule for the use of standard subdivisions.

(2) **Dictionary of Commerce**

381 = Commerce (Trade)

Add as instructed fewer than 380

–03 – Dictionary SS (T1)

380.01-09 – Standard Subdivision

381 + 03 = 381.03

(3) **Dictionary of Botany**

580 – Botany (Plants)

580.1-9 standard subdivision

–03 – Dictionary SS (T1)

58~~0~~ + 03

Class number = 580.3

(4) **Dictionary of Zoology (Animals)**

590 – Zoology

590.1 – 9 – Standard Subdivision

–03 – Dictionary SS (T1)

59~~0~~ + 03

Class number = 590.3

(5) **Dictionary of Biology**

570 – Biology (Life Sciences)

570.1 – 9 – Standard Subdivisions

–03 – Dictionary SS (T1)

57~~0~~ + 03

Class number = 570.3

(6) **Dictionary of Economics**
330 – Economics
03 – Dictionary SS (T1)
330.01 – 09 Standard subdivisions (use of SS in schedule)
33θ + 03
Class number = 330.03
Periodical of Commerce – 381 + 05
381.05

(7) **Dictionary of Homoeopathy**
615.532 + 03
Class number 615.532 03

(8) **Dictionary of Computer Science**
004 – Computer Science
03 – Dictionary SS (T1)
004 + 03
Class number = 004.03

(9) **Dictionary of Medical Science**
610 – Medicine and Health
–03 – Dictionary SS (T1)
610.1 – 9 – Standard subdivisions
61θ + 03
Class number = 610.3

(10) **Encyclopedia of Human Anatomy**
611 – Human Anatomy
611.001 – 009 – Standard subdivisions
–03 – Encyclopedia
611 + 03
611.003

(11) **Dictionary of Human Physiology**
612 – Human Physiology
612.001 – 009 – Standard subdivisions
–03 – Dictionary SS (T1)
612 + 0 + 03
Class number 612.003

(12) **Dictionary of Private Law**

346 – Private Law

346.001 – 009 – Standard subdivisions

–03 – Dictionary

346 + 003

Class number = 346.003

(13) **Dictionary of Psychology**

150 – Psychology

–03 – Dictionary from SS (T1)

150.1 – 9 – standard subdivisions

15~~0~~ + 03

Class number = 150.3

(14) **Dictionary of Sociology**

301 – Sociology

–03 – Dictionary SS (T1)

301 + 03

Class number = 301.03

(15) **Dictionary of Mathematics**

510 = Mathematics

Dictionary = 03

51~~0~~ + 03

Class number = 510.3

(16) **Dictionary of History**

History = 900

03 – Dictionary SS (T1)

9~~00~~ + 03

Cut the filler zeros

Class number = 903

(17) **Dictionary of Garden Crops**

635 = Garden Crops

–03 = Dictionary

Class number = 635.03

(18) **Dictionary of Fruits**
634 = Fruits
–03 = Dictionary
Class number = 634.03

(19) **Dictionary of Archaeology**
930.1 – Archaeology
–03 – Dictionary SS (T1)
930.1 + 03
Class number = 930.103

(20) **Dictionary of Indian Islands and Adjacent Countries**
91 – Base number for Geography
–54 – India (T2)
–142 – Islands
Under 913 – 919
Add to base number 91 notation 3-9 from Table 2
91 + 54 + 142 + 03
Class number = 915.414 203

## Dictionaries of Literature

(1) **Dictionary of Urdu Literature**
891.439 – Base number for Urdu
03 (T3B) – Standard subdivision under 01-07 (p. 625)
891.439 + 03 = 891.439 03

(2) **Dictionary of American Literature**
81 – Base number for American Literature
03 – (T3B) (SS from T3B)
81 + 03 = 810.3

(3) **Dictionary of American Epic Poetry**
81 – Base number for American Literature
1032 – Epic Poetry (T3B)
03 – Dictionary from SS under –102-107 (p. 628)
Class Number = 81 + 1032 + 03
811.032 03

(4) **Dictionary of Punjabi Literature**
891.42 – Base number for Punjabi Literature

03 – T3B (SS through table 3b) (01-07 = Standard sub divisions, page 625)
891.42 + 03
Class number = 891.420 3

(5) **Dictionary of Hindi Literature**
891.43 – Hindi Literature
03 – Dictionary T3B
891.43 + 03
Class number = 891.430 3

(6) **Serial of English Literature**
82 + 05 (SS through T3B, p. 625, V. 1)
Class number = 820.5

## Reference

1. Pandey, S.K. Sharma, *Practical Approach to DDC*, New Delhi: Ess Ess, 1998, pp. 161-63.

# 10

# Multiple Syntheses

Dictionary meaning of multiple synthesis is that it is a process in which substances combine to form completely new substances. Similarly in DDC when we build a number by adding notations to a base number from various parts of schedules, Tables (1-6), Inner tables in schedule by instructions, a new number is formed, it is called multiple synthesis. Other tables are used only with the permission in main schedules or in Table 1. Table 2, Table 5 and Table 6 are used only when instructed.

T2 is used through SS 09 when there is not any instruction but the title demands area notation. Table 3 (T3a, T3b, T3c) is applied to Literature (800-899). T4 is applied to Languages (400-499).[1]

### Examples

(2) **Anatomy of Dog Heart**

636.7 = Dog

636.7001 – 708 Standard subdivisions, specific topics in husbandry of dogs

Add to base number 636.70 the numbers following 636.0 in 636.001 – 636.08

63.089 = veterinary sciences

Add to base number 636.089 the numbers following 61 in 610-618

611.12 = Anatomy of heart

636.70 + ~~636.0~~89 + ~~61~~1.12

636.708 911 2

(3) **Social Reform Movement against Substance Abuse**

362.29 = (Substance Abuse)

362.2911 – 29109 specific aspects of substance abuse

Add to base number 362.291 notation 1-8 from table under 362-363 (Inner Table of schedule).

5 = Social Action

Instruction: add to 5 the numbers following 361 in 361.2-361.8

361.24 = Reform Movement

362.291 + 5 + ~~361~~.24

362.291 524

(4) **International Action against Narcotics**

*Narcotics= 362.293

This *leads us to add as instructed under 362-363 (Inner Table of schedule).

5 = Social Action

: add to 5 the numbers following 361 in361.2-361.8

361.26 = International Action

362.293 + 5 + ~~361~~.26

362.293 526

(5) **Synthesis of Organic Caesium Drugs**

615.3 = Organic Drugs

615.31 = Synthetic Drugs

Add to Base Number 615.31 the numbers following 547.0 in 547.01-547.08

547.05 = Specific organ metallic compounds

547.053-.057 adds to Base Number 547.05 the numbers following 546 in 546.3–546.7

546.385 = Caesium

615.31 + ~~547.0~~5 + ~~546~~.385

615.315 385

(6) **Administration of Medical Libraries**

025 = Library Operations

025.19-Administration of Specific types of Institutions

Add to Base number 025.19 the numbers following 02 in 026-027

026 = Libraries devoted to specific Subjects and Disciplines

026.001-999 = Specific Subjects and Disciplines

Add to base number 026 the notation 001-999

Medical Libraries = 026 + 610 (p. 65, V. 2)

025.19 + ~~026~~.61~~0~~

025.196 61

(7) **Similarly Administration of Law Libraries**

025.19 + ~~026~~ + 340

025.193 4

(8) **Similarly Administration of Secondary School Libraries**

025.19 + ~~02~~7.8223 (p. 55, V. 2)

025.197 822 3

(9) **Disease of Dogs**

Dogs = 636.7

636.7001-.708 Add to base number 636.70 the numbers following 636.0 in notation 636.001-636.08

636.089 = Veterinary Science (Veterinary Medicine)

Add to base number 636.089 the numbers following 61 in 610-618

616 = Diseases

636.70 + ~~636.0~~89 + ~~61~~6

636.708 96

(10) **Veterinary Viral Disease in Dogs**

636.7 = Dogs

636.7001-.708 = Standard Subdivisions

Add to base number 636.70 the numbers following 636.0 in (636.09-636.08)

636.089 = Veterinary Sciences (Veterinary Medicine)

Add to base Number 636.089 the numbers following 61 in 610-618

616.9 = Viral Disease

636.70 + ~~636.0~~89 + ~~61~~6.9

636.708 969

(11) **Radiotherapy of Cancer of Blood**

*Cancer of Blood = 616.994 18

This star leads us to add as instructed under 618.1-618.8

06 = other therapy

062-069 = other therapies

Add to 06 the numbers following 615.8 in 615.82-615.89

615.842 = Radiotherapy

616.99418 + 06 + ~~615.8~~42

616.994 180 642

(12) **Injuries caused to Potatoes by high temperature**

*Potatoes = 635.21

Asterisk leads us to add as instructed under 633-635

Under 633-635 = 633.635 = Specific Plant Crops (p. 310, V. 3)

9 = Injuries, diseases, pests

Add to 9 the numbers following 632 in 632.1-632.9)

632.12 = Injuries caused to by high temperature and Drought

635.21 + 9 + ~~632~~.12

635.219 12

(13) **U.K. Parliament's Debates**

328 = Legislation

328.4-.9 = the legislative process in specific countries in the modern world

Add areas notation 4-9 from Table 2 to base number 328 and then add further from the special table given under 328.4-.9

02 = Debates

41 = UK

328 + 41 + 02

328.410 2

(14) **Photography of Hinduism Religious Festivals**

778.9 = Photography of Specific subjects

Add to base number 778.9 the numbers following 704.94 in 704.942-704.949

704.948 9 = other religions

Add to base number 704.9489 the numbers following 29 in 292-299

294.5 = Hinduism

294.51-53 Mythology Relations, doctrines, public worship and other practices

Add to base number 294.5 the numbers following 20 in 201-203

203.6 = Religious Festivals

778.9 + ~~704.94~~89 + ~~29~~4.5 + ~~20~~3.6

778.989 453 6

(15) **Young Workers in Clerical Occupations**

331.381 = Young Workers in industries and Occupations

Under 331.381001-381999

Add to base number 331.381 notation 001-999

651.37 = Clerical services

331.381 + 651.37

331.381 651 37

(16) **International Trade of Tobacco**

343.087 = International Commerce in specific commodities

33.0877-.0875

Add to base number 343.087 the numbers following 381.4 in 381.41-381.45

381.41 = Products of Agriculture

381.413-.418 = Specific products

Add to base number 381.41 the numbers following 63 in 633-638

343.087 + ~~381.4~~1 + ~~63~~3.71

343.087 137 1

(17) **International Trade of Oil**

343.087 = International Commerce in Specific Commodities

33.0877-.0875

Add to base number 343.087 the numbers following 381.4 in 381.41-381.45

381.42 = Products of Mineral Industries

381.422-.429 = Specific Products

Add to base number 381.42 the numbers following 553 in 553.2-553.9

553.282 = Oil

343.087 + ~~381.4~~2 + ~~553~~.282

343.087 228 2

(18) **Monkeys as Pests of Plums**

634.22 = *Plums

Add as instructed under 633-635

9 = Pests

Add to 9 the numbers following 632 in 632.1-632.9

632.6 = Animal Pests

Add to base number 632.6 the numbers following 59 in 592-599

599.8 = Monkeys

634.22 + 9 + ~~632~~.6 + ~~599~~.8

634.229 698

(19) **Parrots as Corn Pests**

*Corn = 633.15

Asterisk leads us to add as instructed under 633-635

9 = Pests

Add to 9 the numbers following 632 in 632.1-632.9

632.6 = Animal Pests

Add to base number 632.6 the numbers following 59 in 592-599

598.71 = Parrots

633.15 + 9 + ~~632~~.6 + ~~59~~8.71

633.159 687 1

(20) **Atomic Structure of Plutonium**

546.434 = *Plutonium

Asterisk leads us to add as instructed under546

4 = Theoretical Chemistry

Add to 4 the numbers following 541.2 in 541.22-541.28

541.24 Atomic Structure
546.434 + 4 + ~~541.2~~4
546.434 44
Similarly Magneto Chemistry of Actinium
546.421 + 5 + ~~541.3~~78
546.421 578

(21) **Radio Chemistry of Thorium**
546.422 = *Thorium
5 = Physical Chemistry
Add to 5 the numbers following 541.3 in 541.33-541.39
541.38 = Radio Chemistry
546.422 + 5 + ~~541.3~~8
546.422 58

(22) **Cases Involving International Trade of Rice**
343.087 = *International Commerce (Foreign Trade)
343.0871-.0875
Add to base number 343.087 the numbers following 381.4 in 381.41-381
381.41 = Products of Agriculture
381.413-381.418 = Specific Commodities
Add to base number 381.4 the numbers following 63 in 633-638
And then add further as instructed under 342-347
633.18 = Rice
Asterisk on *International Commerce leads us to add as instructed under 342 – 346
0264 = Cases (from table under 342-346)
343.087 + ~~381.4~~1 + ~~63~~3.18 + 0264 (e.g. on p. 568, V. 2)
343.087 131 802 64

(23) **Administrative Regulations on Labor Law in Developing Countries**
344.1 = Law of Socio Economic Regions
Add to base number 344.1 the numbers following -17 in Notation 171-177 from Table 2 and then to the result

add numbers following 344 in 344.001-344.09 then add as instruction under 342-347 (p. 585, V. 2)

–1724 = Developing Countries (T2)

Labor Law = 344.01

0263 = Laws and Regulations

344.1 + ~~17~~24 + ~~344~~.01 + 0263

344.124 010 263

(24) **Cases involving Child Labor Law**

In this title at first we will get classification number for

*Labor Law = 344.01

Child Labor Law and then by adding from (331.01-331.8)

Cases = 0264 (inner table under 342-347)

Labor Law = 344.01

344.011-.018 = Specific aspects of Labor Law (e.g. p. 575, V. 2)

Add to base number 344.01 the numbers following 331 in 331.1-331.8 and then add further as instructed under 342-347

331.31 = Children Workers

0264 = Cases (from Table under 342-346)

344.01 + ~~331~~.31 + 0264

344.013 102 64

(25) Cases Involving in International Crime of Hijacking

345.02 = *Crimes

345.023-.028 = Specific crimes and classes of Crime

Add to base number 345.02 the number following 364.1 in 364.13-364-18

364.1552 = hijacking

345.02 + ~~364.1~~552

345.025 52 = International Problem of Hijacking

Asterisk on Crime leads us to add as instructed under 342 – 346

0264 = Cases (from Table under 342-346)

345.02 + ~~364.1~~552 + 0264

345.025 520 264

(26) **Cases involving Automobile Insurance**

346 = Private Law

346.086 = Insurance Law

346.0860-.0869 = Risks and Sales Grouping

Add to base number 346.0860 the numbers following 368.0 in 368.06 – 368.09 and then add as instructed under 342-347(p. 602, V. 2)

368.092 = Automobile

0264 = Cases (under 342 – 347)

346.0860 + ~~368.0~~92 + 0264

346.086 092 026 4

(27) **Laws and Regulations for Fire Insurance**

Insurance = 346.086

346.0861-0868 = Specific topics of Insurance

Add to base number 346.086 the numbers following 368 in 368.1 –368.8 and then add further as instructed under 342-347 (p. 603, V. 2)

368.11 = Fire Insurance

0263 = Laws and Regulations (Under 342-347)

346.086 + ~~368~~.11 + 0263

346.086 110 263

(28) **Indian Law of Marriage**

Private Law = 346

346.3-.9 = Add to the base number 346 notation 3-9 from Table 2 then add to the result the numbers following 346 in 346.001-346.09

54 = India (T2)

346.016 = Marriage Law

346 + 54 + ~~346~~.016

346.540 16

(29) **Finance Ministry of India**

352.4 = Financial Administration and Budgets

There is no instruction to add area directly in schedule but the title demands area. So we will add area through standard subdivision 09 from Table 1.

–09 = SS (T1)
54 = India
352.4 + 09 + 54
352.409 54

(30) **Home Ministry of Bangladesh**
353.3 = *Administration of services related to Domestic order (Home Ministry)
–09 = (T1)
–5492 = Bangladesh
353.3 + 09 + 5492
353.309 549 2

(31) **Effects of high Temperature on Cells**
571.63 = Cell anatomy, morphology, biophysics, culture Under 571.634
Add to base number 571.63 the numbers following 571 in 571.401-571.49
571.467 = High Temperatures
571.63 + ~~571~~.467
571.634 67

(32) **Secretions in Digestive System**
573.3 = *Digestive System
Asterisk leads to add as instructed under 573
3 = Anatomy and general biological processes of system 33-39
Add to 3 the numbers following 571 in 571.3-571.9
571.79 = secretion
573.3 + 3 (from inner table under 573) + ~~571~~.79
573.337 9

(33) **Cinematography of Birds**
778.538 = Cinematography of Specific Subjects
Add to base number 778.538 notation 001-999 (e.g. p. 645, V. 3)
598 = Aves (Birds)
778.538 + 598
778.538 598

(34) **Remodeling of Psychiatric Hospital Building**

*Psychiatric Hospital Building = 725.52

Asterisk leads us to add as instructed under 721-729

0286 = Remodeling (Under 721-729)

725.52 + 0286

725.520 286

(35) **Architectural Drawings of Public Library Buildings**

727.8 = *Library Buildings

Under 727.821-.828 = Specific kinds of General Libraries

Add to base number 727.82 the numbers following 027 in 027.1-027.8

027.4 = Public libraries

Asterisk leads us to add as instructed under 721-729

0222 = Architectural Drawings (Pictures and related illustrations) (p. 559, V. 3)

727.82 + ~~027~~.4 + 0222

272.824 022 2

(36) **Energy Conservation System in National Library Building**

727.8 = *Library Buildings

727.821-828 = Specific kinds of General Libraries

Add to base number 727.82 the numbers following 027 in 027.1-027.8

027.5 = National libraries

This asterisk (*Library Buildings) leads us to add as instructed under 721-729.

04 = Special Topics (As under 721-729)

Add to Base number 04 the numbers following 720.4 in 720.47-720.49

720.472 = Energy conservation

04 + 720.472

727.82 + ~~027~~.5 + 04 + ~~720.4~~72

727.825 047 2

(37) **Solar Energy System in School Library Building**

727.82 + ~~027~~.8 + 04 + ~~720.4~~73

727.828 047 3

(38) **Buddhist Monasteries**

726.7 = Monastic Buildings

726.78 = Monastic Buildings of orders of other religions

Add to base number 726.78 the numbers following 29 in 292-299

294.3 = Buddhism

726.78 + ~~29~~4.3

726.784 3

Similarly

(39) **Architecture of Monastic Building of Hindus**

726.7 = Monastic Buildings

726.78 = Monastic buildings of orders of other religions

Add to base number 726.78 the numbers following 29 in 292-299

294.5 = Hinduism

726.78 + ~~29~~4.5

726.784 5

(40) **Mythology and Legend in Iconography**

731.8 = *Iconography

731.82-.89 = other specific subjects

Add to base number 731.8 the numbers following 704.94 in 704.942-704.949

704.947 = Mythology and Legend

731.8 + ~~704.94~~7

731.87

(41) **Techniques of Landscape Painting in Water Color**

751.422 = *Water color painting

751.4224 = Water color painting techniques by subject

Add to Base number 751.4224 the numbers following 704.94 in 704.942-704.949

704.9436 = Landscapes (p. 624, V. 3, DDC 22)

751.4224 + ~~704.94~~36

751.422 436

(42) **Draped Figures in Oil Painting**

751.45 = Oil painting

751.754 = Oil painting techniques by subject

Add to base number 751.454 the numbers following 704.94 in 704.942-704.949

704.9422 = Draped Figures (p. 624, V. 3, DDC 22)

751.454 + ~~704.94~~22

751.454 22

(43) **Nudes in Chinese Ink Painting**

751.4251 = Chinese ink painting

751.42514 = Chinese ink painting techniques by subject

Add to base number 751.42514 the numbers following 704.94 in 704.942-704.949

704.9421 = nudes (p. 624, V. 3, DDC 22)

751.42514 + ~~704.94~~21

751.425 142 1

(44) **Postal Stamps of Plants of the World (p. 636, V. 3)**

769.56 = Postage stamps and related devices

769.564 = Postage stamps depicting various specific subjects (iconography)

Add to base number 769.564 the numbers following 704.94 in 704.942-704.949

704.9434 = Plants (fine and decorative art)

769.564 + ~~704.94~~34

769.564 34

(45) **Photography of Still Life**

778.9 = Photography of specific subjects

Add to base number 778.9 the numbers following 704.94 in 704.942-704.949

704.9435 = still life (p. 542, V. 3)

778.9 + ~~704.94~~34

778.934

(46) **Roots of Lilies**

584.3 = *Lilies

Asterisk leads us to add as instructed under 583-588

Under 583-588

1 = general topics in natural History of plants

Add to base number 1 the numbers following 581 in 581.3-581.7

581.498 = Roots

584.3 + 1 + ~~581~~.498

584.314 98

(47) **Stems of Onions**

584.33 = *Onions

Asterisk leads us to add as instructed under 583-588

Under 583-588

Add to base number 1 the numbers following 581 in 581.3-581.7

581.495 = Stems

584.33 + 1 + ~~581~~.495

584.331 495

(48) **Effects of light on Monocotyledons**

571.455 = *Effects of light

Asterisk leads us to go to under 571-572

Under 571-572

Add to each subdivision identified by * the numbers following 571 in 571.01-571.2

571.2 = Plants and micro-organism

571.201-.28

Add to base number 571.2 the numbers following 58 in 580.1-588

584 = Monocotyledons

571.455 + ~~571~~.2 + ~~58~~4

571.455 24

(49) **Effects of Ultraviolet Radiation on Dicotyledons**

571.456 = *Effects of Ultraviolet Radiation

Asterisk leads us to go to under 571-572

Under 571-572

Add to each subdivision identified by * the numbers following 571 in 571.01-571.2

571.2 = Plants and micro-organism
571.201-.28
Add to base number 571.2 the numbers following 58 in 580.1-588
583 = Dicotyledons
571.456 + ~~571~~.2 + ~~58~~3
571.456 23

(50) **Avocado Seeds**
583.23 = *Avocado
Asterisk leads us to add as instructed under 583-588
Under 583-588
Add to 1 the numbers following 581 in 581.3-581.7
581.467 = Seeds
583.23 + 1 + ~~581~~.467
583.231 467

(51) **Similarly Tomato Seeds**
583.952 + 1 + ~~581~~.467
583.952 146 7

(52) **Roots of Figs**
583.45 = *Figs
Asterisk leads us to add as instructed under 583-588
Under 583-588
Add to 1 the numbers following 581 in 581.3-581.7
581.467 = Seeds
583.45 + 1 + ~~581~~.498
583.451 498

(53) **Microscopy in Study of Pollution by Metals**
577.2 = Specific Factors affecting Ecology
577.275 3-.275 7 = Pollution by specific elements and groups of elements
Add to base number 577.275 the numbers following 546 in 546.3- 546.7 and then to the result add standard subdivision Notation as modified under 577.01-577.09
546.3 = Metals

Standard subdivision Notation as modified under 577.01–577.08

0282 = Microscopy (p. 1129, V. 2)

577.275 + ~~546~~.3 + 0282

577.275 302 82

(54) **Pollution by Thorium**

577.275 + ~~546~~.422

577.275 422

(55) **Ecology of Atlantic Ocean**

577 = Marine Ecology

577.73-.75 = Ecology of specific Ocean and Seas

Add to base number 577.7 the numbers following 16 in notation 163-165 from Table 2.

577.7 + ~~16~~3 (T2)

577.73

(56) **Food Chains in Atlantic Ocean (p. 1137, V. 3)**

577 = Marine Ecology

577.375 = Ecology of Specific Ocean and Seas

Add to base number 577.7 the numbers following 16 in notation 163-165 from Table 2, and then add 0 and to the result add the numbers following 577 in 577.01-577.2

–163 = Atlantic Ocean (T2)

0 = Connecting Symbol

577.16 = Food Chains

577.7 + ~~16~~3 + 0 + ~~577~~.16

577.730 16

(57) **Effect of Pollution on Microorganisms**

579 = Microorganisms

579.17 = Ecology, Organisms Characteristic of Specific Environment

.171-.178 Specific Topics in Ecology, Specific environments

Add to base number 579.17 the numbers following 577 in 577.1-577.8

577.27 = Effects of Pollution on Ecology

579.17 + ~~577~~.27

579.172 7

(58) **Effects of High Temperature on leaves of Onions**

571.467 = *Effects of high Temperature

Asterisk leads us to add as instructed under 571-577

Under 571-577

Add to each subdivision identified by * the numbers following 571 in 571.01-571.2

571.2 = Plants and Microorganisms

571.201-.28

Add to base number 571.2 the numbers following 58 in 580.1-588

584.33 = * Onions (onions are monocotyledons)

Asterisk leads us to add as instructed under 583-588

Under 583-588

Add to base number 1 the numbers following 581 in 581.3-581.7

581.48 = Leaves and Fronds

571.467 + ~~571~~.2 + ~~584~~.33 + 1 + ~~581~~.48

571.467 243 314 8

(59) **Effects of Low Temperature on seeds of Lilies**

571.464 = *Effects of Low Temperature

Asterisk leads us to add as instructed under 571-577

Under 571-577

Add to each subdivision identified by * the numbers following 571 in 571.01-571.2

571.2 = Plants and Microorganisms

571.201-.28

Add to base number 571.2 the numbers following 58 in 580.1-588

584.3 = *Lilies

Leads us to add as instructed under 583-588

Under 583-588

Add to base number 1 the numbers following 581 in 581.3-581.7

581.467= *Seeds

571.464 + ~~571~~.2 + ~~584~~.3 + 1 + ~~581~~.467

571.464 243 146 7

(60) **Physical Diagnosis of Dengue Fever in Children in India**

618.92 = Children

Under 618.921-929 = Specific Diseases

Add to base number 618.92 the numbers following 616 in 616.1-616.9

616.91852 = * Dengue fever

As it is asterisk follow instructions under 616

Under 616

075-079- Diagnosis (p. 86, V. 3) inner table of Schedule

Add to 07 the numbers following 616.07 in 616.07-616.079

616.0754 = Physical Diagnosis

Use of SS as modified under 616

009 = Historical and geographical treatment

-54 = India

618.92 + ~~616~~.91852 + 07 + ~~616.07~~54 + 009 + 54

618.929 185 207 540 095 4

# 11

# Titles from Geography and Travel, Biographies and History

## Geography and Travel

(1) **Physical Geography of Forests**

910.021 = physical geography of areas, reasons, places in general

Add to base number 910.021 the numbers following –1 in notation 11-18 from Table 2

910.021 + ~~1~~52 (T2)

910.021 52

(2) **Similarly the Physical Geography of Mountains**

910.021 + ~~1~~43 = 910.021 43

(3) **Physical Geography of Desert Areas**

= 910.021 + ~~1~~54 = 910.021 54

910.1 = Tropical Geography

(4) **Economic Geography of British Isles**

910.1 = Topical Geography

Add to base number 910.1 notation 001-899 and then add 0 add to the result add notation 1-9 from Table 2.

910.1 + 33~~0~~ + 0 + 41

910.133 041

(5) **Explorations by Great Britain**

910.9 = Historical, Geographic, Persons Treatment

910.93-99: Add to base number 910.9 notation 3-9 from table

42 = Great Britain

910.9 + 42

910.942

(6) **Historical Map of India**
911 – Historical Geography
.1-.9 – Geography and persons treatment
Add to base number 911 notation 1-9 from Table 2
**911 + 54 = 911.54 (Historical Map of India)**

(7) **911 + 51 = 951.51 (Historical Map of China)**

(8) **Maps of Western Hemisphere**
912.19 – Specific area, reasons, places in journal
Add to base number 912.19 the numbers following –1 in notation 11-19 from Table 2
–1812 = Western Hemisphere (T2)
912.19 + 1812 = 912.198 12 (p. 841, V. 2)

(9) **Maps of Arabian Sea** = 912.19 + ~~1~~6537 = 912.196 537
Map of India = 912 + 54 = 912.54

(10) **Map of Punjab** = 912 + 54552 = 912.545 52
Under → 913-919 – Geography and travels in ancient and specific continents, countries, localities in modern world
Add to base number 91 notation 3-9 from Table 2
↓

(11) **Geography of England**
91 + 42 = 914.2

(12) **Telephone Directory of Kashmir**
91 + 546 + 003 (table under 913-919)
915.460 03

(13) **Gazetteers of United States**
91 + 73 + 003 (table under 913-919)
917.300 3

(14) **Discovery of America**
91 + 73 + 04
917.304

(15) **Resorts in United States in Bill Clintons Time (1993-2001)**
Resorts = 917.3062
917.30621 – 30629 = Historical Periods

Add to base number 917.3062 the numbers following 973 in 973.1 – 973.9

973.929 – (Bill Clintons Time)

917.3062 + ~~973~~.929

917.306 292 9

(16) **Bed and Breakfast accommodations in USA**

917.3064 = Bed and Breakfast accommodations

Under 917.30641 – 30649 = Historical Periods

Add to base number 917.3064 the numbers following 973 in 973.1 – 973.9

973.929 = (1993-2001)

917.3064 + ~~973~~.929

917.306 492 9

(17) **Facilities for Travelers in England in 2001**

91 = Base number

42 = England

06 = Facilities for Travelers (As instructed under 913-919)

061 = Historical Periods (inner table)

Add to 061 the historical period numbers following 0 that appears in subdivisions of 930-999

941.086 (see instruction under 942.06-942.08)

Add to base number 942.0 the numbers following 941.0 in 941.06-941.08

91 + 42 + 06 + ~~0~~61 + ~~941.0~~86 (p. 843, V. 3)

914.206 186

## Biographies

(A) **Biography as a discipline**

Class biography of persons associated with a specific discipline or subject, plus notation 092 from Table 1

Biography of Chemists = 54 Ø + 092 = 540.92

Biography of Indira Gandhi = 32 Ø + 092 = 320.92

(B) **Biography of ethnic and national groups**

e.g. Biography of Swedes

920.0092 = Biography of national ethnic group

Add to base number 920.0092 notation 05-9 from Table 5

–397 = Swedes

920.0092 + 397 = 920.009 239 7 (p. 848, V. 3)

(C) **General collections of biography by specific continents, countries and localities but not associated with specific subject**

India Who's Who

920.03 - .09= General Collections of Biography by Specific Continent

Add to base number 920.0 notation 3-9 from Table 2

e.g. Collections of biographies of persons resident in England

920.0 + 42 = 920.042

India who's who = 920.0 + 54 = 920.054

(D) ***Biographies of persons with other subjects**

Biography of Astrologers

Base number = 920.9= persons associated with other subjects

Add to base number 920.9 notation 001-999

e.g. Biography of Astrologers

Astrologers= 133.5

920.9 + 133.5 = 920.913 35

(E) **Biographies by historical periods**

Base number = 920.00901-.00905

e.g. General Biographies of 19th century

Base number 920.00901-920.00905

Add to base number 920.0090 the numbers following 090 in notation 0901-0905 from Table 1

19th century = 09034

920.0090 + ~~090~~34

920.009 034

1. **History with respect to ethnic and national groups**

There is an instruction as follows:

Add to base number 909.04 notation 05-9 from Table 5, e.g. World History of Jews 909.04924; then add 0* and to the result add the numbers following 909 in .1-9098, e.g. World History of Jews in 18th century 909.0492407.

There is an option: class here general history of ethic and national groups in a specific continent, country, and locality, prefer subdivision 004 from table under 930-990. If option is chosen, add notation 05-99 from Table 5 as above; then add 00 instead of 0 as above for world history by period, e.g. 909.04924007; for a specific areas add 0 and to the result add notation 3-9 from table

(1) e.g. history of Jews in Germany = 909.04924043.

909 = World History

04 = History with respect to ethnic and national groups

924 = Jews from Table 5

0 = Connecting symbol

43 = Germany from Table 2

909.04 + 924 + 0 + 43

909.049 240 43

(2) **World History of Specific areas, regions, places in general**

History of Tropical Regions in 20th Century = 909. 093082

Instruction: add to base number 909.09 the numbers following –1 in notation 11-19 from Table 2, e.g. History of tropical regions 909.093 of Caribbean Sea 909.09 + 365 (365 from 1365 tropical regions Table 2) then add 0* and to the result add the numbers following 909 in 909.1-909.8, e.g. History of tropical regions in 20th century 909.093082

Explanation of this number

0* = Connecting symbol according to instruction.

82 = 20th Century (from 909.82 p. 835, V. 3)

909.090

909.09 = base number

13 = Tropical Regions (T2) (3 from 13)

(-4-9) History of Modern World: extraterrestrial worlds

909.09 + ~~1~~3 + 082
909.093 082

(3) **History of England**
9 + 42 = 942

(4) **History of India** = 9 + 54 = 954

(5) **History of Punjab** = 9 + 545 52 = 954.552

(6) **History of Medieval India**
954 + 954.02 (Medieval India 647-1785)
954.02

(7) **History of Muslim India**
954 + 954.022 (period of Muslim Conquests, 997-1206)
954.022

(8) **History of Mughal India**
954 + 954.025 (1526-1707)
954.025

(9) **History of British India**
954 + 954.03 (1785-1947)
954.03

(10) **India under Atal Bihari Vajpayee**
954 + 954.053 (1999)
954.053

Formula for history in above titles is
9 + [(Continent + Country) from area table) + Time period from schedule.

(11) **History of Kashmir**
9 + 546 (T2)
= 954.6

# 12
# Options

There are number of options in DDC to serve the needs beyond those represented in a Standard English Language edition. At a number of places in the schedules and tables, options are provided to give emphasis to an aspect in library's collection not given preferred treatment in the standard notation. In some cases, options are also provided to give shorter notation for the aspect.

Options are provided throughout the classification to emphasize jurisdiction, ethnic or national group, language, topic or other characteristics. Options described in notes appear in parenthesis and begin with "option". Options that apply to the full entry appear at the end of the entry. Options to a specific instruction in the entry are intended under the appropriate note.

Same optional numbers are enumerated in schedules and tables and appear in parenthesis in the number column. A special optional arrangement (222)-(224) for books of Bible as arranged in Tanakh as a subsection of the manual note for 221.

Arrange alphabetically and arrange chronologically notes are not placed in parenthesis, but are also options. They represent suggestions only; the material needs not to be arranged alphabetically or chronologically. An example of "arrange alphabetically" note is found at 005.133 specific programming languages: "arrange alphabetically by name of programming languages, e.g. C++".

Some national libraries and central cataloguing authorities assign a few optional numbers. National Library of Canada uses C810 for Canadian Literature in English and C840 for Canadian Literature in French. Most of the time the responsibility for implementing an option rests with the local library. Libraries should weigh the value of using an option against the loss in interoperability of numbers. The library will not be able to use optional numbers assigned by the other library. In addition, unless the option is widely used in a region, users may be confused by the alternate notation.

### Bibliography

016 – Bibliographies and cataloguing of works on specific subjects or in specific disciplinary.

Add to base number 016 notation 001-999.

Bibliographies of computer programme and software 016 + 005.3

**(1) 016 – Bibliography**

005.3 – Computer programme and software

016 + 005.3 = 016.005 3

**(2) General Encyclopedic Works**

016 – Bibliography

03 – Encyclopedia

016 + 03 = 016.03

**(3) Encyclopedia of philosophy = 016 + 01 = 016.1**

**(4) Bibliography of serial publications on philosophy**

016.1 – Philosophy

05 – Serial

But 016.1 not 016.05

**Option:** We can also use 016 as a standard subdivision.

**(5) Bibliographies of medicines = 610.16**

610 – Medicine

016 – Bibliography

61θ + 016 = 610.16

**(6) Reading and use of other information media by children three to five**

028.53 = Reading and use of other information media by specific age groups

Add to 028.53 the numbers following 083 in notation 0832-0835

0833 – Children three to five

028.53 + ~~083~~3

028.533

(7) **Similarly 028.53 + ~~083~~4 = 028.534**

031- General Encyclopedia works in specific works in specific languages and language families.

There are two options for a work, e.g. Arabic Language encyclopedia.

**Option A:** In order to give local emphasis and a shorter number to encyclopedias in a specific language, place them first by use of a letter or by symbol, e.g. Arabic Language Encyclopedia = 03A

039 = General Encyclopedic works in Italic, Hellenic, Other Languages

927 = Arabic Language (T6)

**Option B** = 039.927

= 039.927

039 = general encyclopedia works in Italic, Hellenic, other languages

Add to base number 039 notation 7-9 from Table 6

–927 = Arabic Languages (T6)

039 + 927

= 039.927

051-059 – General serial publications in specific languages and language families

### Hindi—Language Serial Publications

**Option A:** If you want to give local emphasis and a shorter number to serial publications in a specific language. Place them first by use of letter or other symbol e.g. Hindi Language serial publications.

05 H

**Option B:** Arrange serial publications alphabetically under 050

**Option C:** 059-General serial publications in Italic, Hellenic, other languages

Add to base number 059 notation 7-9 from Table 6.

–91431 – Standard Hindi

059 + 91431

059.914 31

060 – General Organizations and Museology

### Organizations in Pakistan

**Option A** = To give local emphasis and a shorter number to organization in a specific country, place them first by use of a letter or other symbol

06 + P

06P = Organizations in Pakistan

**Option B** = 068 + 5491(T2) = 068.549 1

**Option A:** General Organizations in North America = 061

061.3 – General Organizations in United States

### Organizations in Ohio

Add to base number 061 the numbers following –7 in notation 73-79 from Table 2

–771 = Ohio (T2)

061 + ~~7~~71

061.71

**Option B:** 068 general organizations in other geographic area

Add to base number 068 notation 1-9 from Table 2.

Comprehensive works in general organizations in Middle America

–72 – Middle America

068 + 72

= 068.72

**Journalism**

071-079 – Geographic treatment of journalism and newspapers

071 – Journalism and newspaper in North America

**Option A:** To give local emphasis and a shorter number to newspapers and journalism in a specific country, place them first by use of a letter or other symbol.

Newspapers in New Zealand = 07N [preceding 071]

**Option B** = Arrange newspapers alphabetically under 070

**Option C** = to give local emphasis and a shorter number to journalism and newspapers in a specific country other than the United States and Canada, Class them in this number.

**Journalism in North America**

079 – Journalism and newspapers in other geographic Areas.

Add to base number 079 notation 1-9 from T2

–7 = North America

079 + 7 = 079.7

For Canada and United States

Journalism and newspapers in Canada Class in 071.1

Journalism and newspapers in United States class in 071.3-9

Journalism and newspapers in India

**Option A** = 070 (Arrange Alphabetically) (p. 90, v. 2)

**Option B** = 079.I

**Option C** = 079 + 54 = 079.54

**080 = General Collections in specific languages and language families**

**Option A** = to give local emphasis and a shorter number of collection in a specific language, place them first by use of a letter or symbol.

Collections in Urdu = 08U

**Option B** = Arrange collection alphabetically under 080

**Option C** = is given under 081

081 – General collection in American English

089 – General collection in other languages

Add to base number 089 notation 7-9 from Table 6

Chinese language collection = 089 + 51 = 089.51

181.181.9 – Philosophy of specific places

Comprehensive works in 181

Options – to give local emphasis and a shorter number to philosophy of a specific country use one of the following:

**Option A** – Place it first by use of a letter or other symbol.

e.g. Philosophy of Lebanon = 181.L

**Option B** – Class it in 181.1; in that case class comprehensive philosophy of India = 181.4

**Option C** = 181.I

190 = Modern Western and other non-eastern philosophy

**Option A** – Philosophy of Mexico = 19M (to give local emphasis and a shorter number to philosophy of a specific country

**Option B** – Philosophy of Mexico = 199 + 72 = 199.72 (p. 155, V. 2)

Philosophy of Canada and United States = 199.7

**Religion**

290 – Other Religions

Limited to specific religions other than Christianity

Class Religion in general, comprehensive works. Religions other than Christianity in 200; class specific aspects of Religion in 201-209

**Option A:** Class the Religion in 230-280, its sources in 220, comprehensive works in 200; in that case classes the Bible and Christianity in 298.

**Option B:** Class in 210, and add to base number 21 the numbers following the base number for the Religion in 292-299

e.g. Hinduism = 210

Mahabharata = 21 + 294.5923 (Mahabharata = 294.5923) (294.5 = Base no. for Hinduism)

= 219.23 (p. 261, V. 2)

**Option C:** Class in 291 and add the base number 291 the numbers following the base number for that religion in 292-299

e.g. Hinduism = 291

Mahabharata = 291 + ~~294.5~~923

= 291.923

**Option D:** Class in 298 which is permanent ally unassigned

**Option E:** Place first by use of a letter or other symbol

e.g. Hinduism = 2H0 or 29H (preceding 291 or 292)

Add to the base number thus derived, e.g. 2H or 29H, the numbers following the base number for the religion in (292-299)

e.g. Shivaism = 2H + 294.5513

2H = base number for Hinduism

294.551 3 = Shivaism (p. 261, V. 2)

### Options in Law

Under 342-349 branches of law; laws, regulations, cases; law of specific jurisdiction, areas, socio-economic regions.

Classification numbers for law of specific jurisdictions and areas are built from five elements.

Five elements for law numbers.

(1) 34 = Base number, indicating law

(2) A digit indicating specific branch of law, original materials or comprehensive works, under 342-349

(3) The facet indicator 0*

(4) One or more digits indicating or subject subordinate to specific branch of law or type or original material

(5) Notation from Table 2 indicating the jurisdiction or area.

BN + Specific branch + 0 + subject subordinate to a Specific Branch of law + Area

e.g. criminal law of Australia = 34 + 5 + 0 + 1

345.01

To show comprehensive works on a specific jurisdiction or area in modern world; arrange the elements as follows

Base number = 34

Digit indicating comprehensive work = 9

Jurisdiction of area = 94

34 + 9 + 94 = 349.94

**Option A:** to show a specific branch, a specific subject or a kind of material arrange the elements as follows:

Base number = 34

Branch of law; criminal law = 5

Area of Jurisdiction Australia = 94

Facet indicator = 0*

Subordinate subject in branch of law; courts = 1

34 + 5 + 94 + 0 + 1

345.940 1 (Law limited to a specific area or jurisdiction is classed under the jurisdiction before indicating the subject of a branch (p. 547, under –093-099, V. 2)

**Option B:** to give local emphasis and a shorter notation to law of a specific jurisdiction or areas

Base number = 34

Branch of law: criminal law = 5

Facet indicator = 0*

Subordinate subjects in the branch of law; courts = 1

34 + 5 + 0 + 1

345.01 (Smaller number)

**Option C:** to give preferred treatment to jurisdiction in general, arrange elements as follows

e.g. criminal courts in Australia

Base number = 34

Branch of law; criminal law = 5

Subordinate subject in branch of law: courts = 1

Facet Indicator = 0*

Jurisdiction or area: Australia = 94

34 + 5 + 1 + 0 + 94

345.109 4

**Criminal Courts of India**

**Option A** – to give local emphasis and shorter notation

34 + 5 + 01 = 345.01

**Option B** – to give preferred treatment to jurisdiction in general

34 + 54 + 0 + 5 + 1

345.405 1

**Option C** – to give preferred treatment to branch of law and its subordinate subjects

34 + 5 + 1 + 0 + 54

345.105 4

Another Option = Law of Education

Education = 370

–026 = Laws, regulations, cases, procedures, courts (Table 1)

370 + 026

370.26

(Class the law of a specific discipline or subject the specific discipline or subject, plus notation 026 from Table 1 (SS) (p. 547, V. 2)

351 – Public administration

351.076

Civil service examination in specific subjects

See the subject, + notation –076 from 657 + –076 (T1)

657 = Accounting

–076 = Civil Service Examination (T1)

657 + 076

657.076

Table 1

Examinations in accounting = 657.076

**Option:** class here civil service examination in specific subjects prefer the subject in 001-999, plus 076 from Table 1. If you chose this option, add to base number 351.076 notation 001-999

Civil Service examinations in accounting

351.076 + 657

351.076 657 (p. 623, V. 2)

Under 351.3-.9 – Administration in specific continents, countries, localities.

Use 009 – historical, geographic, person treatment

Used for geographic treatment only when area of interest is narrower than area of jurisdiction

**Option A:** United States federal administration in Gulf coast states of USA

351 – Public Administration

–73 – United States

009 – S.S. (under p. 624, V. 2)

–76 = Gulf coast States (V. 1)

351 + 73 + 009 + 76 = 351.730 097 6

351.7300976 Option A: Option A: class treatment of specific topics of Public administration by specific continents, countries, localities in 351.3-351.9

e.g. Public Administration in Germany

Public Administration = 351

Add to base no. 351 notation 3-9 from Table 2

–43 = Germany

351 + 43 = 351.43 option A

**Option B:** In order to give local emphasis and shorter notation, class specific topics of Public Administration treated in jurisdictions, requiring local emphasis in 352-354 without adding 09 from this table and class specific topics of Public administration in specific continents, countries, localities not requiring local emphasis in 351.03-351.9

e.g. Local Administration in Germany

352.14 – local Administration

–09 –5.5 (from Table under 352-354)

–43 = Germany

352.14 + 09 + 43 = 352.140 943

378.4-9- higher education in specific continents, countries, localities, in modern world higher education

e.g. higher education in Mexico

378-Higher education

Add to Base no. 378 notation 4-9 from Table 2

–72 = Mexico (T2)

378 + 72 = 378.72

**Option:** If it is desired to give local emphasis and a shorter number to a specific college or university, place it first by use of a letter or other symbol.

e.g. university of South Africa = 378.S (proceeding 378.4)

University of Mexico = 378.M (p. 823, V. 2)

Language = 400

492.7 = Arabic Language

To give local emphasis and a shorter number to a specific language, place it first by the use of a letter or other symbol.

e.g. Arabic language = 4A0 (proceeding 420), for which the base number is 4A

Class number for Punjabi Language = 491.42

According to option = 4P0

For Hindi Language = 491.43

According to option = 4H0

Hindi grammar = 4H + 5(T4)

4H5

780 – Music

This schedule does not distinguish scores, texts or recordings.

Option: to distinguish scores, texts, or recordings, use one of the following:

(**Option A:** Prefix letter or other symbol to the number for treatises: e.g. scores for violin M787.2, violin recordings R787.2 or MR787.2; use a special prefix to distinguish miniature scores from other scores, MM7872.

(**Option B:** Add to the number for treatises the numbers following 78 in 780.26-780.269, e.g. miniature scores of music for violin 787.20265)

(**Option C:** Class recordings in 789, e.g. recordings of folk music 789.2, recordings of violin folk music 789.2072). Under 781-788 principles, forms, ensembles, voices, instruments class music of all traditions.

(**Option:** 781-788 may be used for only one tradition of music in that case, class all other traditions in 789. If it is desired to emphasized western art music class if here and class all other traditions of music in 789, e.g.

Jazz 789.5; or it is desired to emphasize Jazz, class it here and class all other traditions of music in 789, e.g. western art music 789.8.

(789) Composers and traditions of music

(Optional number and subdivisions; prefer 780-788)

(**Option A:** Arrange treatises about all composers at 789 plus an alphabetic mark; then to the result and notation following 78 in 780-788.)

(**Option B:** Use 789 and its subdivisions for traditions of music.)

(**Option C:** Use 789 and its subdivisions for recordings of music if option A is used with either option B or C, Class comprehensive works on traditions of music in 789.1.)

Unless other instructions are given, class a subject with aspects in two or more subdivisions of 789 in the number coming last, e.g. Spanish folk music springtime 789.261015242 (not 789.2015242).

### Literature

810-890 literatures of specific languages and language families.

Literature is classed by the language in which originally written.

**Option:** class translations into a language requiring local emphasis with the literature of that language.

**Option:** for any group of literatures, add notation 04 from Table 1 and then add 01-89 from table 3b, e.g. collection of literary texts written in Ethiopian languages = 892.80408. Other options for specific groups of literature are found at 891.4, 894.8, 896, 897, and 898.

**Option:** to give preferred treatment to, or make available more and shorter numbers for the classification of literature of any specific language that it is desired to emphasize, use one of the following options.

(**Option A:** class in 810, where full instructions appear.)

(**Option B:** give preferred treatment by placing 810 through use of a letter or other symbol, e.g. literature of Arabic language 8A0, for which the base number is 8A, p. 733, V. 3.)

810.1-818- subdivisions of American literature in English class comprehensive works in 810.

**Option C:** distinguish literatures of specific countries by Initial letters, e.g.:

Literature of Canada = C 810

Literature of Jamaica = J 810

Literature of United States = U 810 or class literature not requiring local emphasis in 819.

Literature = 800

In order to give local emphasis and a shorter number to the literature of a specific language, place it first by the use of a letter or other symbol

| | |
|---|---|
| | 891.42 = Punjabi literature |
| **Option:** | 8P0 = Punjabi literature |
| | 8P1 = Punjabi Poetry |
| | 8P2 = Punjabi drama |
| | 8P3 = Punjabi Fiction |
| | 8P4 = Punjabi Essays |
| | 8P5 = Punjabi Essays |
| | 8P6 = Punjabi Letters |

8P7 = Punjabi Humor and Satire

8P8 = Punjabi miscellaneous writings

This short notation can be written easily on the slim spines of the books.

**History**

909.04 – History with respect to ethnic and national groups.

Add to base no. 909.04 notation 05-9 from Table 5

e.g.: World history of jews in 18th History = 909.0492407

(**Option:** class here general history of ethnic and national groups in a specific continents, countries, locality, prefer subdivision 004 from table under 930 – 990. If this option is choosen, add notation 05 – 99 from Table 5 as above, then add 00 instead of 0 as above for world history period.

e.g.: World History of jews in 18th century = 909.04 + 924 + 00 + 909.7

= 909.049 240 07 (p. 833, V. 3)

**Economic geography**

910.1 = Tropical geography

Add to base no. 910.1 notation 001-899

330 = 910.1 Economics

910.1 + 330

910.133

Option C (optional number; prefer specific subject)

330 + 910 = 330.91

920.1 – 928

**Biography of specific classes of persons**

(**Option A:** use subdivisions identified by *

(**Option B:** class individual Biography in 92 or B; class collected biography in 92 or 920 undivided.)

(**Option C:** class individual Biography of men in 920.71; class individual Biographies of women in 920.72.)

(Prefer specific discipline or Subject, plus notation 092 from Table 1.)

e.g.: Collected Biographies of Scientists = 509.92

934 – India to 647 (Ancient History of India)

(Option: class in 954.01)

Add to Base number 954.01 the numbers following 934.0 in 934.01 – 934.07

e.g.: reign of Ashoka = 954.01 + 934.045

= 954.014 5

935 – Mesopotamia and Iranian Plateau to 637

(**Option:** class Mesopotamia in 956.701; class Iranian Plateau in 955.01.)

943.012 – Ancient History to 481

(Optional number; prefer 936.3)

943.0121 – Early History to 113 B.C.

(Optional number; prefer 936.301)

934.0122 – Period of Contacts with Roman Republic and Empire, 113 B.C.-481 A.D.

(Optional number; prefer 936.302)

CENTRAL ASIA = 958

(**Option:** class here early history to ca.640: prefer 939.6.)

958.01-04 – Historical Period

Add to base no. 958.0 the numbers following 950 in 950.1 – 950.4

e.g.: Period of Mongol Empire = 958.02

In (Area) Table 2

Under -4-9 Modern World; extraterrestrial worlds

(**Options:** To give local emphasis and a shorter number to a specific country, place it first under its own continent or major region by use of a letter or other symbol.)

e.g. Pakistan – 5P [preceding –51]; then sub-arrange each such number like the corresponding number in this table

e.g. Peshawar = 5P23, apply like any other area notation

e.g. Geology of Peshawar = 555.P23

History of Pakistan since 1971 = 95P.05

History of medical Sciences in Pakistan = 610 + 95P

610.95P

Option on page number 238 of Table 1

# Bibliography


*Classification Theory and Practice*, University School of Open Learning Chandigarh, P.U., Chandigarh, 2016.

*Dewey Decimal Classification Theory and Practice,* Indira Gandhi National Open University, New Delhi, 2005.

*Dewey Decimal Classification and Relative Index/Devised* by Melvil Dewey. 22nd ed./edited by John S. Mitchell, et al. Dublin: OCLC, 2003, 1-4V.

Kaushik, S.K., *DDC 22nd A Practical Approach*, New Delhi: Ess Ess, 2004.

Morctimer, Mary, *Leain DDC 22*, USA: Total Recall Publication Inc., 2007.

*Pustakalya Classification Practice, DDC*, 19th Ed., V. 2, IGNOU, New Delhi.

Satija, M.P., *Dewey Decimal Classification: Exercises in the 22nd Edition*, New Delhi: Ess Ess, 2004.

Sharma, C.K., *Dewey Decimal Classification: Practical Handbook*, New Delhi: Atlantic Publishers and Distributors (P) Ltd., 2004.

Sharma, S.K., *Pandey Practical Approach to DDC*, New Delhi: Ess Ess, 1998.

Taylor, Arlene G., *Introduction to Cataloguing and Classification*; Chapter 10 Decimal Classification, 10th edition, mess: Libraries unlimited, 2006.

www.oclc.org/dew